# Letters Home
## 1944-1945

## Women Airforce Service Pilots
## World War II

## Bernice "Bee" Falk Haydu

Edited by Rita Cody Casey
Foreword by Sally Van Wagenen Keil

*Flying experiences of a young woman and her determination to remain a pilot throughout her life.*

FRONT COVER:
1944—Picture of the author about to embark on a flight in a PT-17 Stearman, a primary training aircraft.

Wings—the lozenge (diamond) in the center of the wings is the Greek symbol of womanhood. The male pilots had a different shield in the center of their wings, the symbol of manhood.

Fifinella—the good luck lady gremlin designed by Walt Disney for the WASP. She rode the wingtips of the hundreds of women pilots who flew alongside their brother airmen as part of America's air armada of World War II.

BACK COVER:
Bee in WASP uniform.
This photo and the picture of Joe and Bee in chapter 16 were taken by Mort Kaye of Palm Beach, Florida.

email: beehaydu@beehaydu.com

May 2009 Congress passed a Bill to award the Congressional Gold Medal, the highest civilian award in the United States, to all the WASP for their service in World War II. March 10, 2010 Medals were given by Congress at a ceremony in the Emancipation Room at the Capitol.

2010 4th Edition
ISBN 0-9747675-3-0

*Always blue skies.*
*Bee*

*Bernice Falk Haydu*

# Letters Home
# 1944-1945

*To the memory of my beloved mother*
*who had the foresight to save my letters*
*written in 1944 and 1945.*

*For my wondeful husband, Joseph, and*
*our children Joe, Steve and Diana*
*who have lived through my WASP*
*stories for many years.*

# CONTENTS

# FOREWORD

While I was a girl growing up in post World War II America and imagining what I could do when I grew up, I had an advantage. Both my grandmothers were college graduates, my mother a specialist in early childhood education, my aunt a doctor and, most evocative of all in my girlish mind, my Aunt Mary had flown huge B-17 bombers during the war with the WASP. She herself was larger than life to me, being five-foot-eleven, dynamic, stylish and an executive at Macy's Department Store in New York. I assumed every girl had an aunt like her and knew all about the WASP.

Then, suddenly, soon after I myself landed in New York as a journalist and graduate student, she died. Grown up now, I had so many questions to ask her about what the WASP had been like when she was my age. I wanted to know all about what she had done and could no longer ask. No one seemed to know anything about the WASP of World War II. This sent me on a personal quest that led me, over the course of the next five years, to the living rooms of former WASP all over the country to ask them questions I could never ask her. One day in 1977, I took a bus ride from New York to New Jersey and the bus driver let me off right at the driveway of the home of WASP Bee Falk Haydu and her husband Joe. Their daughter, Diana, appeared, and we all spent many hours late into the evening hearing about Bee's experience with the WASP.

I was particularly pleased to meet, Bee, not just because meeting a WASP was always an honor, and not just because I knew I would get to have a wonderful time with another spirited, energetic, highly intelligent and attractive woman in her '50s, professionally active, in Bee's case still flying, but because she was just the kind of woman I was attempting to become. Bee not only had made history, she was doing so again at that very moment.

As I was learning more about these amazing women who flew airplanes for the war effort–I now had a book contract urging me to ask my questions–I found myself an eye witness to history, as my generation of American women caught up with the WASP thirty years later when they became the focus of a Congressional fight worthy of a miniature D-day. In 1944 the U.S. Congress had refused to bring the WASP formally into the military, as it had the WAC and the WAVE, also originally civilian 'experiments' to see if women could do military jobs. The idea of women flying airplanes was more than Congress could accept in 1944. Could it now in 1977? Women were finally being accepted into the service academies and again for military pilot training, but few knew it was 'again.' The WASP, now numbering upwards of 900 strong, were determined to get Congress to pass legislation giving them their full military status and recognition at last. They declared 1977 The Year of the WASP and descended on Washington to fight for their cause.

History this time was made not as the 'first women' in the cockpits of B-l7s and P-47s. Now the WASP were to be political pioneers. This meant smart, sophisticated political action. The way to do this was shown them by Colonel Bruce Arnold, son of General H. H. "Hap" Arnold, the head of the Air Force in World War II, who had promised them his capable assistance. Once again, the WASP would show 'em it should be done and how. I found myself there to see and report first-hand on an unexpected culminating chapter in my book, called, of course, *The Year of the WASP*. I assumed they would be victorious; hadn't we come a long way, baby? I had no idea how brilliantly, strategically, valiantly, concertedly they would have to fight, 30 years later, to take Capitol Hill.

In the fall of 1975 the WASP had elected a president who would lead their legislative charge fifty-five year-old Bernice "Bee" Falk Haydu. Did she have any idea what turbulence she was heading into? The WASP motto, I'd often been told, was "What's next?" and if anyone embodied that spirit, it was Bee Haydu. For over two years, Bee donned her chic WASP uniform (the WASP were the first to wear Air Force blue) and, with focus, determination and, that ineffable political asset charm, she networked the halls of Congress. She devoted herself to organizing, motivating, rallying her 'troops,' who came to Washington in uniform making the Senate and House Veterans Affairs Committee rooms a sea of Santiago blue on hearing days. Congress has not heard more expert and impressive testimony than they heard presented by the Women Airforce Service Pilots of World War II.

How could 900 or so women in their 50s and 60s scattered around America even imagine trying to get a bill through the United States Congress? Because they were WASP. And also because they had Bee as their president. Bee wrote her membership (and everyone else she could think of) reams of letters and news bulletins, organized a nationwide petition campaign and called relentlessly for documentation showing that their military service was official in all but imprimatur. Over my many trips to Washington, Bee kept me informed, as I was by then assigned by a women's magazine of the time to write an article on the WASP and their fight for national recognition. As I interviewed, took notes and wrote, I watched as Bee and her WASP colleagues came forth with that prodigious WASP ability and spirit all over again. To my amazement and horror they again faced incomprehension and opposition in Congress. The opposition astounded me. After thirty years, the WASP were being made to prove not only that they could do what they did, but that they had done it. They got heavyweight supporters–Senator Barry Goldwater, Colonel Bruce Arnold, Congresswoman Lindy Boggs, Congresswoman Margaret Heckler (later Cabinet Secretary), Antonia Chayes, Assistant Secretary of the Air Force and many others.

I already knew two things about the WASP, for which I was inexpressibly grateful, and for which they would thank themselves. They worked together with effectiveness and mutual respect like no other group of women I had ever seen to get the job done. And they remembered. The country may have forgotten what they had done (or worse; official reports I found on the WASP in the Air Force Historical Office were stamped TOP SECRET), but the WASP had not. They all seemed to have scrapbooks in Army trunks in which they saved everything from those two or three remarkable years of their lives. Congress made them show proof beyond any doubt that their military service was truly military.

Today, interviewed, filmed, published and sought after as speakers, the WASP have attained truly legendary status and continue to bring stars to the eyes of generations of women in the military, women flying for airlines and air charter companies and all the rest of us who are their legatees. My book on the WASP was published in 1979. Reissued in a 2nd edition, it is still in print. When I first interviewed Bee, I was the age she and the WASP were when they trained in Sweetwater and flew their wartime missions as AAF pilots. Today, I am the age Bee was when she helped lead the WASP to win official recognition as World War II veterans. For me, history is life, life is history. My Aunt Mary Parker, Bee and all the WASP have inspired me not only to write and to fly, but to fly straight into life till that last flight.

Sally Van Wagenen Keil

# PREFACE

I am a Bee wannabe. When growing up I loved flying and read all about Jacqueline Cochran and the WASP. I had taken a few flying lessons when the war started ending my lessons. Too young to be a WASP, I read everything I could find about them. Years later when I met Bee Haydu and learned that she was a WASP I said to her, "I wanted to be you?"

We met after we had both retired to Florida. We played golf together on ladies' days and became friends. One day she mentioned that she had given the Texas Women's University in Denton, Texas, the original letters she had written home. Another time she told us that she was going up North to be inducted into the Aviation Hall of Fame & Museum of New Jersey. Our local newspaper ran a wonderful article about her that impressed all of us who knew her mainly as a golfing buddy.

In the meantime Bee and I would talk about flying. Two of my sons and one grandson are pilots. One son is a 777 captain with American Airlines and has also written and published a book. Bee's husband, Joe, was a flight instructor in the Army Air Force during the war and my husband, Moe, was in the Naval Air Service, we had so much to talk about it was difficult to concentrate on golf. The more Bee and I talked the more I realized that her story was a fascinating and significant part of aviation history especially important in this year celebrating the Wright Brothers' first flight centennial.

We started with the letters that her mother, bless her, had saved and that I just loved reading because I lived the life of a WASP vicariously through these wonderful letters. The warmth and love of her family show through her letters and those of her brother, Lloyd. We are privileged that her mother saved these missives and that Bee and Lloyd are willing to share them with us.

While reading the letters I would ask Bee to expand on the stories and explain different terms. Her technical knowledge is awesome. As she expanded on one story it led to another.

After we finished the letters I said, "Then what happened?" Her tales of trying to find a job in flying after the war were enlightening and I loved her experiences selling airplanes as a dealer for Cessna. Being a former real estate broker/sales manager and wife of a sales manager I think everyone in sales will admire her skill and perseverance in cold calling, setting goals and reaching them.

Who would imagine that two such aviation-minded people as Bee and Joe would meet, fall in love, have a family, and spend the next fifty plus years enjoying flying? How many husbands would be so supportive, sponsor his wife's air races, join in flying contests with her, and help teach their children to fly? They were made for each other! Their passion for flying added a fervor and cohesiveness to their family that nothing else could! They are unique!

Chapter 13 gives us all pause for thought. This was truly Bee's luckiest day!

Chapter 14 will be a shock and an eye-opener to those who think the nation appreciated these women and thanked them for their sacrifice for their country when they were disbanded. Bee was president of the WASP at the time when they were fighting for recognition. I asked her to expand on that because I didn't know what that entailed. After she explained, penned the facts and dug out the newspaper articles and pictures I realized she was one of the prime movers, and organizers of the terrific battle the WASP had to wage to gain recognition as veterans from the United States Senate and House of Representatives. Colonel Bruce Arnold, son of General "Hap" Arnold thanked Bee personally for her tremendous help in leading the WASP through her two terms as president to the final victory in Congress. Joe and their children sustained her all the way.

"Looking Back"–Bee wondered what her family and friends felt about her lifelong commitment to flying and was thrilled with their answers.

"Summing Up"–She and they would do it all again!

I delighted in reading Bee's stories, sometimes challenging, sometimes exciting, always interesting and discovering that I had a real aviation heroine as a friend. She has spanned the hundred years of aviation history as an active participant from the days of the Stearman biplane to the space shuttle.

Bee is currently the historian for the Women Military Aviators, Inc. and on the Aviation Advisory Board of Palm Beach County.

*Letters Home 1944–1945* by Bernice "Bee" Falk Haydu is a must read for everyone, especially aviation buffs.

Rita Cody Casey
Editor

# ACKNOWLEDGMENTS

Texas Woman's University, Denton, Texas, where the original letters were transcribed and are currently preserved in the WASP archives at that university. They have an engrossing website that I am sure you would enjoy– www.twu.edu/wasp.

Sally Van Wagenen Keil for her foreword and whose book *Those Wonderful Women in Their Flying Machines: The Unknown Heroines of World War II* was one of the very first books detailing the accomplishments of the WASP. In May 1977 a condensed version was printed in Viva, the international magazine for women. Information about her book may be obtained by telephoning 1-800-556-6200.

How can I find the right words of praise for my wonderful friend, Rita Casey? In addition to being a good friend, she has been the most enthusiastic, encouraging, persevering, knowledgeable, talented person I have ever known. Wrapped in this one person was an editor, collaborator, consultant and proofreader. When she was not sure of something, off she went to the library to find books for her research. She spent hours 'tweaking' sentences as well as clarifying some of my writings. I shall be ever grateful for her help.

Maurice Casey, Rita's husband, was invaluable as a photo enhancer. His skill and patience were inestimable. I thank him for the magic he performed with his computer on my old snapshots and pictures.

My son, Joseph, who in a weak moment said to son Steve and daughter, Diana "Let's get Mom a computer!" They did, although they may be sorry now. He, Steve, Diana, son-in-law Jeff, friends Jane and Gene Montanaro and others too numerous to mention, have given me computer help on many occasions.

All gave willingly of their knowledge and skills.

Of course my most important and enthusiastic booster was my husband, Joe. He endured hours of listening to my frustrated outcries as I would suddenly discover that what I had just finished writing had either disappeared or gone 'somewhere' in the computer–never to be found.

# INTRODUCTION

The unprovoked Japanese attack on Pearl Harbor December 7, 1941, led to the United States entrance into World War II. Both aircraft and pilots were in short supply. Jacqueline Cochran, an accomplished, well-known and highly decorated woman pilot approached President Franklin D. Roosevelt with the idea of utilizing women pilots in the war effort. Initially the president was hesitant since the thinking at that time was that women belonged in the home.

By September 1942 the need for pilots to ferry aircraft from factory to points of embarkation and to Air Force training airports was desperate. Nancy Love, another talented woman pilot, was asked to establish the Women's Auxiliary Ferrying Squadron or WAFS at New Castle Army Air Base, Delaware, under the Air Transport Command. Their primary duty was to deliver aircraft. The requirement for each of the twenty-eight women accepted in that group was that she have a minimum of 500 hours of flying experience.

At around the same time Jacqueline Cochran's offer to organize a group of women pilots was accepted by Army Air Force Commanding General H. H. "Hap" Arnold and the Women's Flying Training Detachment or WFTD was started at Houston Municipal Airport, Houston, Texas. In April 1942 they transferred to Avenger Field, Sweetwater, Texas. The idea was to enlist women pilots with less experience than was required by the WAFS.

Initially the requirement was for two hundred hours of flying time but as the experimental program progressed the required hours were reduced to thirty-five. Initially the training was six months and was similar to that of male cadets. The group was funded by Civil Service. Once the program was deemed successful the intention was to make the women a part of the Air Force and the training was eventually increased to seven months.

In June 1943 the name was changed to Women Airforce Service Pilots or WASP, Jacqueline Cochran, Director. The WAFS were included, with Nancy Love remaining as Commander of the Ferrying Service.

More than 25,000 women from all over the United States, Canada, England and Brazil applied for training. Those who were not United States citizens were automatically rejected. Of these applicants, 1,830 were accepted 1,074 won their wings. After graduation they were assigned either to the Ferry Command or the Training Command where they towed targets for infantry to practice with live bullets, flew missions for tracking, smoke laying, searchlight strafing and simulated bombing, tested radio controlled aircraft, were flight instructors, did engineering test flying, were utility pilots and performed all stateside flying duties.

Since they were formed to relieve male pilots for active duty General Arnold did not want the WASP to go overseas. They flew every aircraft manufactured for World War II including the B-29, that dropped the atomic bomb on Hiroshima.

In 1944 General Arnold went before Congress to seek approval to make the WASP a part of the Army Air Force. By this time our desperate need for aircraft and pilots had been fulfilled. Men were needed in the Infantry. The male pilots in this country had no desire to be called into that branch of the service and lobbied for the disbanding of the WASP making untrue accusations and generating adverse publicity. Consequently the WASP were disbanded December 20, 1944, having been defeated by nineteen votes in the House of Representatives.

This is a collection of excerpts from my letters home in 1944 and 1945 while serving in the Women Airforce Service Pilots and immediately thereafter. It includes several letters from my brother Lloyd who served in the Army Air Force as a meteorologist in England and France. He was involved in the weather predictions so important in determining D-day. My wise mother saved all of our letters.

Aviation became an important part of my life.

After the war, I made it my civilian career. When I married Joseph Haydu, who had been a flight instructor in World War II, he owned several Army surplus planes. He used some of them for banner towing. I believe he was the first to start this type of advertising in New Jersey.

Flying became a hobby we both enjoyed and shared with our children and grandchildren. We attended many air shows and competitions and Joe always encouraged me to participate in women's air races. I have chronicled some of the races and flying adventures we have experienced over the years.

When the WASP reorganized and struggled to be recognized as veterans by the government, the fight culminated during my term as president of the organization. I devoted an extraordinary amount of time alerting our membership, planning strategy, forming committees, arranging publicity, and preparing for and testifying before Congress. This involved many trips to Washington, D. C. and across the country. Joe and our children were extremely supportive.

**We all celebrated when we were finally**
**recognized as Veterans of World War II.**

Bernice "Bee" Falk Haydu

# Letters Home
## 1944-1945

# ONE

# <u>LEARNING TO FLY</u>

Frequently, I am asked how my parents felt when I decided to fly. After reviewing the accomplishments of my ancestors, it is not surprising that they were supportive and enthusiastic about my choice.

On my father's side my grandmother, Jennie Calisher Falk, and grandfather, Henry Falk, were both born in the United States to parents of German descent. My grandfather was in the dressmakers' supplies business in Manhattan where he and a partner had four locations. Later they moved to Bradley Beach, New Jersey, where he established a haberdashery shop in addition to his New York City businesses. His wife, Jennie, liked dabbling in the stock market, leading to her downfall in the crash of 1929. This was usually the domain of men, so you can see that she was a woman ahead of her time.

My grandmother on my mother's side, Sadie Rosenthal, came to the United States with her family as a young teenager. My grandfather, Leopold Blum, came here alone at the age of thirteen. Both came from Germany in the 1880s and met and married here in America. After raising a family of four, Sadie established a pleating and embroidery business, which blossomed into a hemstitching and dressmakers' supplies business. Grandfather Blum, who had been a salesman for a dry goods and window shade establishment, worked with her and helped her expand her business. He also served as a justice of the peace in Newark, New Jersey for many years.

My mother, Della Blum, at the age of twenty-one established branches of the family's hemstitching and dressmakers' supplies business in Montclair and East Orange, New Jersey. She turned these over to her father after her marriage to Leroy Falk in 1918.

My father served a short time in the United States Army in 1918.

After they married, Leroy and Della owned a women's lingerie shop in Asbury Park, New Jersey, but eventually moved to Montclair. In 1925 they opened a lingerie and costume jewelry shop called the Vanity Box. Leroy also sold real estate in New Jersey and in Florida. In 1928 he entered the taxicab business with the Twentieth Century Cab Company, an owners' cooperative, and at one time owned four taxicabs. When the depression came my mother was forced to close the Vanity Box. She was not a quitter and her earnings were needed so she opened the Montclair Employment Agency, which she managed from our home. She also rented out rooms in our large house.

On December 15, 1920, I was born into this industrious family where the women were emancipated and enjoyed the freedom to work and help earn money for their families. They were independent and wanted to succeed. They were not constrained by the Victorian idea that women shouldn't work outside the home or that some occupations were available only to men.

The young Falks welcomed me into the world in their house at Bradley Beach, New Jersey. In those days, doctors came to the house to deliver babies. My brother had been born a year earlier in Ocean Grove. My sister, Jacqueline Joan, was born in 1932.

When I was three we moved to Montclair where I went to school from kindergarten through high school. I was graduated in June 1938. The economy was still feeling the effects of the depression and it was difficult to get a job, especially for a woman. I knew during high school there would not be enough money to send both my brother and me to college so I took mainly courses preparatory to becoming a secretary, one of the few jobs open to women.

Job-hunting was so competitive that in order to get the want ads early, I would travel by bus from East Orange where we were living at the time to Newark to get the *Newark Evening News* 'hot off the press.'

It was not until the fall that I finally found employment at the George F. Mack real estate office in East Orange. When Mack lost a large management contract he had to let me go. My next job was with Cronheim, another real estate office, in the real estate management division. (Little did I realize that this training would come in handy for investing years later.) Working conditions in this office were not the best. Again, I turned to the want ads and was hired as private secretary to the patent attorney for Conmar, a zipper manufacturer producing zippers for the war effort in Newark.

**By then World War II was a reality.**

The fact that I had been unable to attend college always bothered me. While working for Conmar I thought, *Stop feeling sorry for your self and do something about it.*

When inquiring about night school I was amazed to find courses in aviation. Rationalizing that aviation was here to stay and wanting to do something more for the war effort, especially since my brother was now in the Army Air Force, I made the decision to take courses in aviation. Therefore, in 1943 I enrolled in the aviation course at the Newark College of Engineering, Newark, New Jersey.

### This began my long love affair with flying!

The instructor at the college was Charles Grieder who ran a flight school. This course whetted my appetite for actually flying an airplane. Normally, Grieder's flight school would have been closer to where I lived in East Orange but because of the war a Defense Zone had been established. No private flying was permitted from the East Coast through New Jersey. Charlie had to relocate and opened an airport at Martins Creek, Pennsylvania, just across the Delaware River from Belvedere, New Jersey, some seventy miles west of where I lived.

Since I was working I could only spend time flying on weekends

*Charles Grieder and Bernice Falk at Martins Creek*

*Raising the flag in front of the hangar. Deck on top is where we used to sun ourselves and watch the action.*

and vacations. Having no car, as was the case with most of us attending flight school, on Friday nights I would take a Greyhound bus to Belvedere where Charlie would pick up his students and take them to Martins Creek. He had rented a house on the Delaware River close to the airport so those coming a distance could stay overnight. We each chipped in a nominal sum for food and helped with the housework and cooking.

## Anything to help get us in the air!

Charlie built a hangar that we helped construct when we weren't flying. When the weather was too bad for flying he rigged up a wooden platform that he attached to the back of his car. He would drive slowly up and down the field  while we walked behind picking up stones and placing them on the platform so the airplanes would not be harmed when taking off and landing. Charlie had only four planes so we had to take turns flying. The planes were Taylorcraft with side-by-side seating, 65-horsepower and brakes at your heels. They had to be started by pulling the propeller through by hand. While learning to fly I earned the nickname "Bee." My friends said I flew like a bumble-bee.

Sometimes we did things we were not supposed to do. A pilot with the status of student was not supposed to have anyone else in the plane other than an instructor. My friend, Gen North and I now had Howard Bartholomew–"Bart" as our instructor. He was a mischievous person and suggested we fly together and try some acrobatics (now called aerobatics). We had read about these stunts  but had never attempted to  perform. them. One day when Gen was scheduled to fly solo, Bart suggested I hide in the wooded section of the airport that she had to taxi past before takeoff. She stopped and I sneaked into the plane. We climbed to a safe altitude and attempted a loop, a maneuver that has the aircraft go straight up, over on its back and then return to the straight and level position. We decided that I

*Bee, Bart and Gen. We had to wear parachutes when doing acrobatics.*

6

would handle the wheel (some small aircraft had a stick) and she would take the rudder. We failed in the maneuver but enjoyed ourselves immensely and succeeded in landing safely, a surprise since we were laughing so much.

A big milestone in learning to fly is your first solo flight.

## My first solo was on August 1, 1943.

Before attaining your pilot's license you must prove your proficiency by flying a solo cross-country flight. If you have ever flown in the northwest area of New Jersey you know there are many rolling hills. One rolling hill soon looks the same as the next rolling hill. On my first solo cross-country it didn't take me long to realize I was lost. Worried about running out of fuel I searched the area below and saw a lovely, long field, a nearby church and a pub. I landed on the grass turned off the aircraft and went into the pub to find out where I was and to calculate how to get back to the airport. Planning to do just that and not mention I was lost, I returned to the aircraft with a few pub patrons to help me get the plane started. Since we had no electric starter and the propeller had to be pulled through by hand I asked one of the men to sit in the plane and hold the brakes while I pulled the prop through. Try as I might, the engine would not start. Much to my embarrassment I had to phone the airport and admit my dilemma. They promptly flew to my rescue and wouldn't you know the engine started up immediately. It probably just needed to cool down!

Years later I learned that the field is still being used by the residents of the Millburn Estate for their friends who have airplanes. The town is called Tranquility and the pub is currently a very fine restaurant. How lucky can you get? A church on one side of the road a pub on the other and a perfect landing strip with the airplane and pilot unharmed–chagrined maybe, but thankfully, unharmed.

Among those of us taking flying lessons at Martins Creek six applied and were accepted in the WASP class of 44-7. One of the requirements was 35 hours of flying time.

After applying, we were interviewed by Mrs. Ethel Sheehy, Jacqueline Cochran's representative. If accepted we had to take and pass the Army Air
Force physical for pilots, supply character references and get release forms from our current employers if we had a defense related job. Mine was defense related.

Once approved and assigned a class we traveled to Sweetwater, Texas, the location of the training school, at our own expense. If we failed any part of the seven-month training program we had to return home, again at our own expense. Most who failed (washed-out) did so in the primary phase of training.

*January 1944 farewell party given in the hangar at Martins Creek Airport. The six who would be entering the class of 44-7 in Sweetwater, Texas, for WASP training. Marie Lynch, Alice Gartland, Gerry Ashwell, Betty Pettitt, Bernice "Bee " Falk, Winnie Lo Pinto.*

In January, 1944 General Arnold recommended amendments to the proposed legislation which would make possible WASP to be directly commissioned into the Army Air Forces. Deputy Chief of Air Staff thought militarization might be affected <u>without</u> legislation. He asked the Assistant Chief/Air Staff personnel to look into the legality of commissioning women pilots directly into the Army on the basis of their qualification as service pilots stating that if such legal basis could be found, General Arnold would be highly pleased because it would be the answer to militarizing the WASP. In his reply the AC/AS personnel cited a decision of the Comptroller General which stated that the authority required extended only to men and could "not be regarded as authority for commissioning women as officers in the Army of the United States".

TWO

## <u>TRAVEL TO SWEETWATER</u>

The six of us who had been learning to fly at Martins Creek decided to make the train trip to Sweetwater together in coach class. Marie Lynch, Alice Gartland, Gerry Ashwell and Winnie Lo Pinto boarded the train at Pennsylvania Station in New York City. Betty Pettit and I joined them on the train in New Jersey. We had to change trains in St. Louis, which resulted in my first letter home.

*Seeing me off at the Train Station in Newark, New Jersey. My mother, Della, sister, Jacqueline, and Opa Blum (Opa–German nickname for Grandfather).*

Wednesday, February 9, 1944

Dear Mom and Everybody,

Well here we are waiting for the train to leave St. Louis. We really had a great bit of luck. When we arrived we saw the government agent (a soldier told us to do this) and he sent a man downstairs to meet us at 4:45– they open the gates for the train for everyone at 5:15–the man let us right on the train and we were able to snare good seats. He also spoke to the Pullman

9

conductor about giving us Pullmans in case of cancellations. I doubt if there will be any but we have our fingers crossed.

Live and learn about traveling, never again by coach if possible. All we did in St. Louis was take a walk for about half an hour and then rush back. We had so many arrangements what with luggage and meeting people that we had no time to waste. But really the people in the station have been just swell to us which is surprising. The station is absolutely immense and it seems to me to be just as busy but much more confusing than Grand Central or Penn Station.

The country during our trip today was very flat and uneventful looking. We noticed that most farms raise pigs–but not the fat waddling type–ones with long thin legs. Last night we evidently passed through the nicest part of the journey. I could see by the moonlight that we went through many mountains and followed the Susquehanna River for quite a while. These were the Alleghenies. I looked for shacks and poor farms but so far we have not passed many at all. On the contrary, the farms and homes looked quite well-kept.

My roast chicken was devoured last night at about 10:00 p.m. and we ate Alice's today.*

We still have sandwiches, cookies, bread, fruit, candy, figs, dates, etc. from six lunches. We expect to have enough food left over to keep us through the first week at Sweetwater. The girls all liked your chicken very much. So far we have only eaten one meal on the train and that was breakfast this morning.

We are about to pull out of St. Louis in a couple of minutes so I'll finish this some other time.

* Our families had prepared delicious box lunches, which we shared, and gratefully devoured on the long train ride.

Friday the 11th

Well here we are in Sweetwater after a good night's sleep and two wonderful baths. I'll pick up from St. Louis.

We left, and much to my surprise, this last half of the trip was not nearly as bad as we had anticipated. I slept somewhat on the train that night. I am sure from sheer exhaustion. At approximately 2:30 a.m. the train had about a half hour stop in Little Rock, Arkansas, and a man came thru the car screaming, "Doughnuts! Coffee!" at the top of his lungs and waking everyone. Those of us who did not wake up at that were startled to have a package of doughnuts thrown in our laps by a kind-hearted captain who kept buying us cakes and coffee throughout the whole trip. We drank the coffee, which tasted like last week's dishwater, but was hot and warmed us. After the train started we dozed again. We woke early, washed, dashed into the diner for breakfast and had fun with the captain and other soldiers on the train. All this time the scenery was more or less ordinary. We arrived in Fort Worth at 12:45 and changed to another train that left at 2:10 p.m. (By the way we had changed our watches, setting them back an hour.)

This train was by far the worst but being the last leg of the journey we didn't mind. The beauty of the country more than made up for the inconvenience, plus the fact that we all had seats while many people had to stand. The country is exactly as pictured in the movies–prairies, gulches, cacti, sagebrush etc. One of the interesting things is the way the mistletoe grows from the bark of trees. The trees are just filled with this parasite. I thought of Jackie when I saw this, and if I can get some, will send it to her. Also the cacti are beautiful. I would like to send you one but probably will not have the opportunity to do either of these things.

Honestly, Mom, the country is very beautiful and the air is just wonderful to breathe. Tell Mr. Whitney* I was very disappointed not to have gone through any desert at all nor did we have trouble with dust seeping in the windows. This is probably because it is winter.

The weather is glorious. It's like a cool spring day–very brisk and refreshing. And I have never seen so much sky in my life. We traveled miles without seeing a person but we did pass many shacks in terrible condition. One of the things that thrilled me most was the sight of oil wells somewhere between Texarkana and Fort Worth. There were just hundreds of them and as someone explained to me, they not only pump oil, but natural gas, which is available to the people at no charge because there is such an abundance.

Much to our surprise, we arrived in Sweetwater just five minutes late–at 8:40 last night. These Texans are really something. Every time we asked the conductor when we would arrive he would say, "Lady, I don't know. We may arrive in five minutes, we may be a day late and we may even go backwards." When the time came for our arrival and we stopped, thinking it was just another stop to wait for a train to pass or something, which is what we had been doing all along, I said to the girls that perhaps we should get our bags together because we might be near Sweetwater. Someone overheard the word Sweetwater and informed us that we were indeed in Sweetwater. There was a mad dash for luggage and scrambling to get out of the train and screaming for a cab and excitement, etc. When we did finally get a cab, we found our hotel was right around the corner from the station.

You should see these Texans. They all wear big hats and many wear boots. Sweetwater is a very lovely place and the people are lovely–very helpful and all. We can hear the planes from here constantly but cannot see them or the field. We heard the planes at 7:30 a.m. It is one steady drone of motors. We had a wonderful breakfast for only $.35 and we found a place where we can have a steak dinner for $.75. We'll try it tonight. I have an idea food down here will be cheap. The trees are still bare but are starting to bloom.

You really have no idea just how big Texas is until you start traveling through. If I can find our timetables, I'll send you the maps. They are off scale, of course, but it will give you an idea of how we came down.

There are many other future WASP here and they all seem to be nice although we have not had a chance to speak to many.

I love to hear the Texans talk although at times it is a bit annoying. Somehow it just sounds false to my ears but I guess that is understandable. They are a very easy-going people and very friendly–something the North so definitely lacks. They really seem to be concerned with you and with helping you. I think I'm going to like Texas very much.

I had better sign off now because we want to take a walk through town. I'm writing lots now because I don't know when I'll have the chance again.

Be sure to send my regards to the Whitneys,* thank Opa again for everything, and you too, dearest Mom.

Love also to Jackie. Take care of yourself.

Love,<br>Bernice

*The Whitneys mentioned are neighbors in East Orange.

*Blue Bonnet Hotel*
*Sweetwater, Texas*

February 11, 1944

Dear Mom and Jake,*

Just found these cards. We have two rooms for three people. The rooms are very large and the beds very soft.

This is the tallest building in town. The air gives one a terrific appetite and we eat day and night. When I get home my clothes will all be too small.

Love,

Bee

*Jake is sister Jacqueline also known as Jackie.


February 12, 1944

Dear Mom,

We are all impatiently awaiting the arrival of the bus to take us to the field. There are about fifty girls scattered in the lobby and about a thousand bags. We were just told that the bus would not arrive until 1:00 p.m. It was supposed to get here at 9:30 a.m. To think we got up at 8:00 all for nothing.

Last night we were invited to the WASP graduation ceremony. It was very impressive.

There was not a lot of speech making and those that were made, were nice and short. The part I liked was that the graduating class sang a song to the other five classes and then each class in turn sang a song to the graduating class. They all had lyrics that had been especially written to some familiar tune. It was very nice.

We had our steak dinner last night and although the meat was tender, it was too thinly cut and not rare. All in all though, it was pretty good. Food around here is cheap.

Our hotel room was only $2.00 a night.

We were amazed to find out that the population of Sweetwater is as high as 15,000. After we went to the roof of the hotel and looked around we could see just how sprawled out the city is. Last night we could not see much of the field because it was so dark. It seems to be rather large and the girls tell us that the traffic is very heavy–planes to the right and left of you.

We saw Pat* and Marge after the graduation  and they look absolutely marvelous. They have so much color in their faces from wind burn that we all look like ghosts compared to them. Gen* wasn't there and we can't imagine where she was. I hope my sending her that box didn't get her in trouble. I'll probably see her today. That's the news up till now.

Love,

Bernice


*Pat Kenworthy Nuckols, class 44-5 and Gen North Mahlbacher 44-6 both learned to fly with us at Martins Creek.

This is the song sung by class 44-1 at their graduation February 11, 1944

## YOU'LL GO FORTH

(Tune: Dig Your Grave With A Silver Spade)

You'll go forth from here with your silver wings
You'll go forth from here with your silver wings
Santiago blue and a heart that sings
'Cause you ain't gonna be here no longer.

Leave your h.p. tricks to the babes in '6'
Leave your h.p. tricks to the babes in '6'
Leave your big city tricks to the gals in the sticks--
'Cause you ain't gonna be here no longer.

You can leave all the drillin' to the W-5 chillun
You can leave all the drillin' to the W-5 chillun
You can leave LaRue's killin' to the gals still
    willin'
'Cause you ain't gonna be here no longer.

Leave your instrument lore to poor W-4
Leave your instrument lore to poor W-4
You can leave all the Links with their gadgets galore
'Cause you ain't gonna be here no longer.

You can leave PT to poor W-3
You can leave PT to poor W-3
You can leave all the cricks from the neck to the knee
'Cause you ain't gonna be here no longer.

Leave your cross-country buzzin' to your W-2 cousin
Leave your cross-country buzzin' to your W-2 cousin
Leave the hedge-hoppin' fun that was W-1.
'Cause you ain't gonna be here no longer.

You'll go forth from here with your silver wings
You'll go forth from here with your silver wings
Santiago blue and a heart that sings
'Cause you ain't gonna be here no longer.

# FIRST WEEKS OF ARMY LIFE

February 14, 1944

Dear Mom,

I'm in the Army now! Can you imagine–here it is 7:50 a.m. and I feel as if I have been up for hours. We rise at 6:00 a.m. (I get up at 6:20) and have breakfast formation at 6:40. We eat and finish about 7:00. As yet we have not been assigned regular duties so they have been giving us thousands of things to do. Once in a while though we have a half an hour or an hour here and there but there are always bays* to clean or some small amount of laundry or something. We have not yet been assigned to regular bays, and are crowded with eight in a bay instead of six. The bays are nice. We have a small cot with a mattress, a locker, a writing desk and a stove. It is plenty warm with the stove except when we first get up. We are responsible for the condition of our bay and get demerits for everything we do wrong. Seventy demerits can eliminate you from the WASP.

We are grouped alphabetically, therefore, I am not in with any of the Martins Creek girls. Everyone is very nice though and since all of us except Betty Pettitt are in Flight 1 (the first half of the alphabet), we can eat together and be together quite a bit.

At this point I was interrupted to fall in so we could get our flight clothes. Since then we have been kept going, and we just finished dinner. Every meal has meat and the food is really good and very plentiful. We will be called again in a few minutes so I doubt if I'll get to finish this.

We were issued 'zoot suit'** (coveralls), outer heavy flying suits, goggles, a helmet, and gloves. I was very fortunate. Yesterday several upper classmen came around and said they had some of their clothes to sell.

I was one of the lucky ones to get there first and this is what I bought, all for only $5.00;

> general's pants***–two pair ($3.95 apiece new)
> summer gym suit,  winter gym suit
> set of winter underwear
> white turbans–two****

I now have just about everything I need except for one or two small items and I haven't even touched your $20.

We do most of our walking to the count of 'hup, tup, threep, four'– translation 'one, two, three, four'. It is quite dark until about 8:00 a.m. and by the time 8:00 a.m. rolls around we feel as if half the day has passed.

Yesterday afternoon we had a test (aptitude) that took about four hours and boy was it tough. Luckily, it is just experimental and our class was the first to take it. It is a test that is actually given to boy air cadets and they want to see how girls react.

I have been falling in and out so often that I completely forget what I have written. I hear we are going to be psychoanalyzed this afternoon.

So long for now and love to all,

Bernice

* Bays–the barracks had separate rooms that accommodated six people. These rooms were called bays.

*Trainees wearing Urban's Turbans*

** Zoot suits were men's suits popular during the early 1940s, characterized by full-legged, tight-cuffed trousers and a long coat with wide lapels and heavily padded wide shoulders. We called the male coveralls that had been issued to us zoot suits. They were anywhere from a male size small to extra large and you wore what was issued.

*** General's pants–officer's pinks was the name of the gabardine dress pants worn by officers. They had no women's slacks so these were issued to us. We renamed them general's pants when it was learned that several generals would be attending a graduation.

**** Urban's turbans–Major Robert Urban, the Air Force commanding officer of our base, decided we should wear covering over our hair. It became mandatory to wear the white turbans, which soon became known as 'Urban's Turbans'.

## WE MARCHED EVERYWHERE

*Parading at one of the graduation ceremonies.*

*Our class marching to ground school around the Wishing Well.*

*Mrs. Leota "Dedie" Deaton, Chief Staff Executive Officer of the WASP, seated on the Wishing Well.*

NOTE: The Wishing Well was an important structure for all of us. We would throw coins in for good luck if we were having a check ride or having difficulty with ground school or any other phase of the training. We would also throw people in the well for an occasion, such as soloing, or throwing in an instructor from ground school when that phase was completed or any other celebration.

General "Hap" Arnold gave us a plaque for the Wishing Well that read:

**March 11, 1944**
**To The Best Women Pilots In The World.**
**General H. H. "Hap" Arnold**

Below is one of the songs we sang to familiar tunes as we marched to various functions.

## ZOOT SUITS AND PARACHUTES
(Tune: Bell Bottom Trousers)
Before I was a member of the AAFTD
I used to be a working girl in Washington, D. C.
My boss he was unkind to me,
He worked me night and day,
I always had the time to work,
But never time to play.
CHORUS
Singing Zoot Suits and Parachutes
And wings of silver, too.
He'll ferry planes
Like his mama used to do.
Along came a pilot, ferrying a plane
He asked me to fly with him down in Lover's Lane
And I, like a silly fool, thinking it no harm
Cuddled in the cockpit to keep the pilot warm.
CHORUS
Early in the morning before the break of day
He handed me a short snort* bill
And this I heard him say,
Take this, my darling, for the damage I have done,
For you may have a daughter, or you may have a son;
If you have a daughter, teach her how to fly,
If you have a son, put the (bleep) in the sky.
CHORUS
The moral of this story as you can plainly see
Is never trust a pilot an inch above the knee.
He'll kiss you and caress you, and promise to be true
And have a girl at every field as all the pilots do.
CHORUS

18

* During WWII a 'short snorter' was a little less than a full drink at a bar. But an aircrew member's 'short snorter' was a chain of paper currency, taped together, end to end, from various countries they had visited. The longer your 'short snorter', the more countries you had visited. Soldiers would have currency signed by comrades much like an autograph book. As one note was filled, another would be connected to the first, usually by tape, with more added as needed. Long 'short snorters' also meant free drinks at the bar, since the person with the shortest one had to buy the round. This tradition began during WWI and heightened during WWII.

*Our 'zoot suits' (male coveralls) which in most cases did not fit as well as these.*

*We ate from metal trays.*

*We started with 8 in a bay but as classes became smaller we had 6. We stored our belongings in the closet and our suitcases under the cots.*

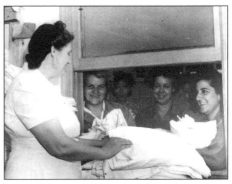

*Once a week we would pick up clean linens.*

February 16, 1944

Dear Mom,

We still have not been assigned to regular bays so we are living out of suitcases.

Yesterday we were psychoanalyzed. There is nothing to it. He just asks you lots of questions about your childhood, home life, attitude, etc. We were also examined by the dentist. He found a cavity–oh me! Other than that we had free time.

Today we are supposed to get our shots–three of them. We had calisthenics–from now on called PT–physical training. This morning we have free time until 12:25. Our eating schedule this week is really screwy. We have breakfast at 6:40, lunch at 12:25 and supper at 8:00.

The girls are all swell. We have quite a variety here. There are a lot of southerners and westerners, and Texans, too. I am not allowed to tell you how many are here, or how many will graduate, so please don't ask.

I may take pictures but I have no film. I would appreciate some Kodak 620 if you can get any. Oh yes, please do not forget to send me my income tax papers. I have been keeping up with my washing and ironing, and sewing of nametapes very well so far.

We have not started flying yet and I doubt if we will for about a week because the other classes are way behind schedule and we have to wait for them to finish. The weather has been kind of drizzly lately.

We don't see Betty Pettitt very often because she is in another flight. We are in Flight 1 the first half, alphabetically, of the class.

I am really very happy and love this life. Of course, we haven't really started to work yet.

Love to all,
Bernice

*Physical training and marching given by Lt. Paul La Rue.*
*To the tune of 'Inky Dinky Parlez Vous' we would sing:*
*Lt. La Rue is winning the war, parlez vous*
*Lt. La Rue is winning the war, parlez vous*
*Lt. La Rue is winning the war with his*
*Hup, Hoo, Heep, Four*
*Inky Dinky Parlez Vous*

Dear Mom,

We were just fingerprinted. Yesterday, we got a third shot the first in a series of three for tetanus. My smallpox shot 'took' and my left arm is a bit sore but will be OK soon. The other shots don't bother me.

This morning we did not have to fall in formation for breakfast and it sure felt swell to sleep until 7:30. Can you imagine! I still have my pajamas on, the red ones, under my zoot suit. About dinnertime–8:00–I'll change my clothes and take a shower. The custom seems to be to wear pajamas all day and save time changing clothes in the morning. You can sleep about five minutes extra.

We started ground school two days ago and have it for three hours a day. So far it's OK. The math and physics instructor is a panic. He talks about everything but the subject, and says he never fails anyone because he doesn't want to make anyone go to study hall.

I am sending you a copy of the paper under separate cover. There is an article* about the exams we took. I shall circle it. Read it to Betty.**

I am busier than ever now because we got an idea for a show*** and I'm on the committee. I have been running from meeting to meeting and doing organizing in my 'spare' time. Lord only knows how it will turn out. Good, I hope. We have been getting special permissions here and there.

   Love to all,
   Bernice

* February 18, 1944, excerpts from *The Avenger*, our newspaper:

"Entrance requirements for the WASP were stiffened last week when all applicants were ordered to take the official Aviation Cadet Qualifying Examination before admittance to the program. The result of the test will become a part of the applicant's official record in WASP headquarters and unless she makes a satisfactory passing grade she will not be called to report for WASP training. W-6 and W-7 trainees already enrolled will be required to take the test also."

In the same issue a quote from Brigadier General Kenneth P. McNaughton, speaker for W-1 graduating class predicted that the WASP program will continue.

"Your job will continue to be the type of non-combat flying which men pilots lack the patience to perform as readily as women."
**Betty Maher, a good friend of mine, had applied for the WASP training but by the time she got her necessary thirty-five hours of flying and submitted her application, it was too late to enter the program. She would have been in

a 1945 class and we were disbanded December 20, 1944.

*** How the *Eager Beaver* show came to be. The class before ours had been held back in their flying because of weather. This meant we could not fly for two weeks, and we had half of each day with nothing to do. I suggested to my classmates that we put on a show giving our first impressions of Army life and demonstrating some of the experiences we were encountering in barracks living. Mrs. Leota Deaton, Chief Staff Executive Officer, agreed that it was a great idea. She asked Julie Jenner (44-3) if she would help us since Julie had been a Ziegfeld Follies girl before joining the WASP. It was

*Mr. James Hill, our mathematics teacher. On the first day he said that none of us would fail his class.*

*We had to practice transmitting and receiving on the radio. We also had to be able to send and receive Morse code at the rate of eight words per minute.*

*Mr. Crawford was our engines instructor*

amazing to discover the many talents of these young women in our class. Some wrote comic skits about visits to the psychologist, our trials undergoing the physical training, our experiences in our bays and the joys of twelve women sharing two showers and two johns etc. Some danced, some played musical instruments and I was elected Master of Ceremonies

February 21, 1944

Dear Mom,

We just got back from PT and boy, what a workout.

Today was a bright one in my life. It was the first day since I have been here that I received any mail. Two letters from you (one of the 16th and one of the 18th), a valentine from Jackie, a very cute one at that and a letter re-addressed here from Sol Winick. Boy, did my morale shoot up! No kidding, I really enjoyed your letters very much. I like to hear all the little pieces of news from home. Could you send me a box of tea balls? You see we have coffee at every meal, as well as milk, of course. For a hot drink I prefer tea once a day. Anyway, too much coffee is not good.

We still have not started flying because the weather, which is very drizzly, is holding back the other classes. However, we are getting our three hours a day of ground school regularly. Our schedule this week permits us to sleep until 6:30 (oh joy), so I get up at 6:45 and put my zoot suit on over my pajamas, and then change my clothes after breakfast.

By the way, I wrote to Lloyd last week. I hope he gets the letter. If his address is changed please let me know.

It seems funny to hear of snow. The sun just came out but there is still a winter nip in the air.

Love to everyone,
and take care,
Bernice

*1943–Bernice with Lloyd, home on leave during training in the United States.*

## Letter from my brother, Lloyd, Stationed in England.

January 11, 1944

Dear Bernice,

I imagine that it is about time for me to start writing you a letter. Probably by the time you get this, you will be in Texas, that is, if you have passed your physical on December 15. It sure is bad to be so far behind on the affairs at home. Probably by the time I hear about the physical news you will be starting your training already. But don't be afraid to stick it out, Bernice. Like in cadet training, they throw the book at you–make it as rough as possible because in the end they want only the best–and I know you won't have too much trouble because you are the best.

Keep me posted on developments. I'll write you more often now since you will not be home and can't get the news from all the letters and the family. But the mail situation is very bad. Two months since I've left home and only one letter from home. The most recent letter I've gotten from anyone–Elea* was written a month ago. But I still have hopes of the mail moving faster. Twice as much space has been reserved for mail in planes flying across to England.

Haven't had much of a chance to visit any of the other places in England since I last visited South Hampton. But I've been enjoying the work we have been doing for the past week or so–practice in operation of weather stations.

I guess I'll just have to be patient about hearing how you are making out in this flying business. I hope you make it without too much trouble.

Good luck, Kiddo,

Love,

Lloyd

*Elea mentioned in this letter is Lloyd's fiancée, Eleanor McCoy, whom he married in September 1945.

Dear Mom,

Well today we have open post, (means we can leave the base) the first since we've been here. But I am not going into town because I have so much to do here. I have letters to write, and should study ground school, as well as cockpit procedure–what you do in the airplane before take off. We have open post because it's raining and that is another reason why I want to stay on post.

We had quite a bit of excitement this morning at about 6:15 a.m. and I slept through the whole thing. It seems a B-17 (Flying Fortress) was trying to land on the field and it was too dark. They were trying to make an emergency landing because at that time we were having a terrific thunder and lightning storm and they feared being hit by lightning more than anything else. They made several unsuccessful passes at the field and tried to reach our tower by radio but no one was in the tower. You see this is not a controlled airport, which means that it is not necessary for someone to be on duty on the radio at all times. To make matters worse, no one knew how to turn on the field lights and those poor boys were just desperately circling the field not able to see a thing or land. Eventually all the girls brought their cars onto the field and the headlights were used to light the runway. The plane finally landed safely much to everyone's joy. The occupants were ten students and one instructor and you can imagine their astonishment on seeing they had landed among all these beautiful girls.

Everyone had a chance to see the ship on the field and get inside it. You have no idea just how big it is. It is the most superb thing I have ever seen and it dwarfed the ships we fly here. All in all, it caused quite a stir in camp and there I slept peacefully on.

I think the reason for this is that my bay is right next to a hangar. The nights in the hangars are spent by cleaning ships, testing motors, shouting workmen, and general confusion, consequently, I am so used to noise while sleeping I can sleep through most anything.

Please do not send me any more pajamas. I have plenty and don't worry about ironing because I hang them in such a position that they dry very neatly and then I only iron the collar. Thanks anyway, for thinking of me. No, Mom, we have not started to fly yet. Yesterday we had pre-flight which consists of meeting your instructor and other personnel on the flight line, learning about filling out forms, being shown cockpit procedure, etc. My instructor is just perfect. Not only is he an instructor, but also a check pilot. I think he will be as strict as the devil but awfully good. I am sure I will like him very much. We were supposed to get our first ride today but came the rain—darn it.

There is nothing to tell you about how I made out on my psych test or any of the others I mentioned in connection with those difficult experimental Air Force tests we had. You see, we never heard anymore about them. The new classes before entering, however, are supposed to take all this stuff and if they 'flunk,' they are not even to come to Avenger. So you see I just got in by the skin of my teeth.

Today, being Sunday, I happened to see a Sunday news funny lying around. It really brought back the memories of our Sundays and all the funny sheets. Remember how busy I used to be and never got to them until the middle of the next week or so? Gosh, now I wouldn't even have a chance to glance at them. It sure brought back memories though.

You know, Mom, I have a feeling I am going to make this course. Lord knows I'm going to work like blazes.

The marks for ground school are posted weekly. Last week I got; 92–engines; 96–math; 90–theory of flight. The ground school is a lot tougher than I thought it would be. They stress that flying comes first, but. I think I should have done better than the above for the week but I have made a vow never to worry about ground school.

Tell me about Jackie and school etc. Some one of these days I'll get around to writing her a letter but with this schedule and show, which is supposed to be put on next Friday, I am rather dizzy as well as busy. Don't know what I'll do when I start flying. Listen, Mom, don't worry and work too hard with the sewing and cooking and cleaning. Please take it easy.

Love to all,
Bernice


Saturday, March 4, 1944

Dear Mom,

Sorry I did not write sooner but my head has literally been going in circles all week. We have been rushing like mad to finish the show for last night, and up to the night before some of the kids had never rehearsed–sheer negligence on the part of many people who were given responsibility. However, we worked hard and produced it last night. It was a great success. As a matter of fact they want us to put it on for Camp Barkeley. *

Your daughter was the Master of Ceremonies. I had no idea from one minute to the next what I was going to say between scenes because I had not written anything or rehearsed, being too busy with managing details. However, everything went off fine and I even told your joke about the man and the two girls who were bats. It went over big. Besides all of this, I have been getting a cold all week, and the day of the show I felt miserable. I didn't fly today nor did I go to town this afternoon but stayed on post and

*Those who were a part of the Eager Beaver show. Alice Gartland (Whitmore), Bernice "Bee" Falk (Haydu), Gerry Ashwell (Lotowycz), Mimi Kerr, Gerry Bowen (Olinger), Julie Jenner (Stege), she was in Class of 44-3 and having been a Ziegfeld Follies girl, had stage experience, Margaret Parish (Garland), Mrs. Helen Shaw 44-7's Class Mother, Lucille Cox, Joan Smythe (McKesson), Edith Upton, Pat Smythe, Beverly Frisbie (Carruth), Dorothy Swain (Lewis).*

FRIDAY, MARCH 17, 1944      THE AVENGER

## W-7's Eager Beaver Show Clicks With First-Night Audience Of 400

### Hilarious Comedy Plays To MRTC Soldiers Friday

To our knowledge, no one ever has rolled in the aisles at a stage comedy—speakingly literally of course . But the audience at W-7's "Eager Beaver" show, March 3, came as near to it as we expect to see of first-nighters. Well · paced, well-acted, and well-staged, its comedy and music went over with a six-gun-like bang, as 450 trainees and a bevy of field officials viewed the "test hop" with approving eyes.

The "Eager Beaver" show, designed by Bee Falk, Joan Gough, Alice Gartland and others in bay A-5 was dedicated to Mrs. Helen Shaw, Class E.O. and Mary Helen Crane, squadron leader. Perhaps most of the credit goes to Bee Falk, promoter, who was selected for Master of Ceremonies and Julie Jenner, W · 3, dramatic critic who patiently "saw it through." Much praise also goes to Kay Kren, Gerry Ashwell, Marie Lynch, Lucille Cox, script writers, Ellen Wimberly, song composer and Scotty Bradley, program and sign painter.

"First Impressions of an Eager Beaver" began with a suitcase scene in the Blue Bonnet Hotel lobby, starring "rum-influenced" Jackie Sherman toting the bottle, chic, fur-draped Bobby Vickers, and "mother" Adelaid Schafer, who cautioned her daughter, Mary Storm, always "to fly low and slow."

Next appeared a quartet with "zoot suit droop" featuring Doris Anderson, Alice Gartland, Ann Cawley and Mimi Caffery.

The second scene, an introduction to the barracks starred Nancy Conklin who brought her corn cob from the Blue Ridge, Bernice Dannefer, fragile southern belle, Beverly ·Frisbie and others.

Between scenes an encore was demanded for "Miss H.P. and a Little Bit More," composed on the flight line by DeRuss Winter and Ellen Wimberly, to Dot Swain's guitar accompaniment.

The next morning in the barracks the Eager Beavers were up a half minute schedule. Grace McElligott had obtained a hudson seal house coat. Gartland had "long reds" and "Blue Ridge" Conklin manipulated to her disadvantage the confounded shower "contraption."

Capt. LaGree, having a mudclehound reputation, could probably make more progress if he would employ the rhythm of talented Joan "Hula" Smythe, one of the biggest hits.

Marv Storm "stole the show" during the gym scene until "epileptic" Norma Trucks took a notion. Other "Amazons" in the scene were Peg "Out-of-step" Parish ,a typical beginner; Alberta Faskvan· as the captain and Frances Winter, drill sergeant.

### All Together (?) - - With A Hup, Tup, Threep, Four!

With questionable coordination and unanimity, Capt. LaGree's physical training class counts out its daily dozen or so in a comic scene from the recently-staged W-7 "Eager Beaver."

After Florida-tanned Mimi Caffery "blued" "Summer Time" and "Stormy Weather," Major Urban's Nightmare slighted to the jazzy tune of "Soldier Stay 'Way From Our Club." The audience howled when Joan Gough, an aggressive trainee, in blue jeans, staggered out with Jenny Gower, the "over-indulgent" instructor. In the corner of the club room a crap game advanced at full pitch. Annie Henry rolled a straight and won Eleanor Gunderson's striped shirt.

In the psycho-scene Ann Cawley, as Dr Buick, was an unruffled psychiatrist who questioned the trainees upon entry to 318 AAFPTD. Mimi Keir as Mimi LaFluff represented the persuasive feminine type. Lizzie Gluzz,

### The Glamour Section

the "well-balanced, too tolerant, emotionally-stable type'" and Agatha Gurgle, the "calm, self satisfied individual," were both expertly portrayed by Lucille Cox. Watching the nervous twitchings of Lucille "Gurgle" Cox gave cases of slight hysteria to several of the audience including E.O.'s Webb and Stires.

We feel sure the repeat performance will get as much applause from Camp Barkeley on March 17, when the show plays to Medical Replacement Training Center soldiers.

Hula-Gal Joan Smythe, Bobby Vickers, and Mimi Caffery (left to right) strike their glamour poses, which added eye appeal (with a raised eyebrow) to W-7's "Eager Beaver" show.

*Ann Cawley as Dr. Buick, Isabella "Mimi" Kerr looking on and Lucille Cox, another patient.*

*Hula Gal, Joan Smythe, Bobby Vickers and Mimi Caffery strike their glamour poses which added eye appeal (with a raised eyebrow) to W-7's Eager Beaver show.*

kept my face in the sun for a couple of hours, slept, and did nothing and I feel much better now.

The weather has been terrible and so far I have only flown twice, two one-hour periods. My instructor Mr. Murray is simply wonderful. He is very strict and tough but he is noted as one of the best on the field. This must be true because he is also a check-pilot, which means I won't be having him very long. As soon as one of the other instructors returns we shall all be turned over to him. I have already tried to see if I could remain with Murray but I think it's impossible.

It's almost time for bed check. Even though this is short I want you to get it soon so I'll sign off now. I received the tea and scissors today and thanks loads. It sure does hit the spot.

How is everything at the store?**
                                    Much love to all,
                                                    Bernice

*Camp Barkeley was the nearby Medical Replacement Training Center.
** The store is Best &Co. where my mother worked.


Quotes from *The Avenger*, March 17, 1944

"The *Eager Beaver* show was instigated by Bee Falk, Joan Gough, Alice Gartland and others in Bay A-5. Perhaps most of the credit goes to Bee Falk, promoter, who was selected for Master of Ceremonies and Julie Jenner W-3 dramatic critic who patiently ' saw it through.'

First impressions of an *Eager Beaver* began with a suitcase scene, in the Blue Bonnet Hotel lobby, starring 'rum-undulated' Jackie Sherman toting the bottle; chic, fur-draped Bobby Vickers and 'mother' Adelaid Schafer, who cautioned her daughter, Mary Storm, always 'to fly low and slow.' Next appeared Doris Anderson, Alice Gartland, Ann Cawley and Mimi a quartet with 'zoot suit droop' featuring Caffery.

The second scene, an introduction to the barracks starred Nancy Conklin who brought her corn cob from the Blue Ridges, Bernice Dannefer, fragile southern belle, Beverly Frisbie and others.

Between scenes an encore was demanded for 'Miss H.P. and a Little Bit More,' composed on the flight line by DeRoss Winter and Ellen Wimberly to Dot Swain's guitar accompaniment. The next morning in the barracks the Eager Beavers were working on a half-minute schedule. Grace

McElligott had obtained a Hudson seal housecoat, Gartland had 'long reds' and 'Blue Ridge' Conklin manipulated to her disadvantage the confounded shower 'contraption.' Capt. LaGree, having a muscle-bound reputation, could probably make more progress if he would employ the rhythm of talented Joan 'Hula' Smythe, one of the biggest hits. Mary Storm 'stole the show' during the gym scene until 'epileptic' Norma Trucks took a notion. Other 'Amazons' in this scene were Peg 'Out-of-step' Parish a typical beginner, Alberta Paskvan as the captain and Frances Winter drill sergeant.

After Florida-tanned Mimi Caffery 'blued' 'Summer Time' and 'Stormy Weather', Major Urban's Nightmare alighted to the jazzy tune of 'Soldier Stay 'Way From Our Club.' The audience howled when Joan Gough an aggressive trainee in blue jeans staggered out with Jenny Gower the 'over-indulgent' instructor. In the corner of the clubroom a crap game advanced at full pitch. Annie Henry rolled a straight and won Eleanor Gunderson's striped shirt. In the psycho-scene Ann Cawley, as Dr. Buick, was an unruffled psychiatrist who questioned the trainees upon entry to 318 AAFFTD. Mimi Kerr as Mimi LaFluff represented the persuasive feminine type. Lizzie Glutz the 'well-balanced, too tolerant, emotionally stable type' and Agatha Gurgle, the 'calm, self satisfied individal' were both expertly portrayed by Lucille Cox. Watching the nervous twitching of Lucile 'Gurgle' Cox gave cases of slight hysteria to several of the audience.

We feel sure the repeat performance will get as much applause from Camp Barkeley on March 17 when the show plays to Medical Replacement Training Center soldiers."


Tuesday, March 7, 1944

Dear Mom,

Besides school, flying, PT, etc., we have been having evening meetings preparing for graduation on Friday and listening to an insurance salesman. I can be  insured for $3,000 during training (six months of training) for $24.75. This is the only type of life insurance that I can get while training. Other insurance can be gotten after I graduate, but right now, that is all. Shall I take it out? I think it would be a good idea. Let me know because I won't do anything until I hear from you.

The show, Friday, was such a success that we have to put it on for Camp Barkeley (a boys camp near here) a week from this Friday.

I have about five hours of flying so far and my instructor has not said anything so I don't know how I'm doing. I guess I told you how wonderful he is. More about that next time.

> Love to all,
>> In haste your dotter,   Bernice

Dear Ma,

I received a gift subscription to Readers Digest from Conmar. *

We were just told tonight that we are having Generals Arnold, Craig, Yount and five other big generals visit us tomorrow for graduation and that is why all the fuss and excitement. It is really quite an honor. Jacqueline Cochran came in today.

Well Mom, the show was such a success that we are going to give it again for Camp Barkeley (a boys camp about twenty miles from here) a week from Friday. I have been acting as Master of Ceremonies.

The graduation** is this Friday, and all week long they have been giving us extra drill, meetings, lectures, etc. and consequently all our free evening time for study and letter writing has been taken up so that I cut my meals short in order to have five minutes here and there to write you and one other letter this week

Yes, I have been hearing from Irv* * *. He sent me a box of candy and wants to send me a gift. He said if I won't tell him what to send (he has been trying to get me a vanity kit but can't find a good one) he will send me a war bond. I really can't help him out. Have you any suggestions? I have also been hearing rather regularly from Sal Winick (the boy I worked with at Conmar who is in Camp Hood, Texas–too far from here.)

Don't worry about me getting on with the girls, or liking them. Sure, they are swell but in a group of over a hundred, you are bound to have one or two who rub you the wrong way. Two of them just happen to be in my bay but there is no outward show of dislike. It is merely that for eating and going out friends I choose others. Please don't take it too seriously. I wrote most of it to give the kids an idea of the partiality of Texans to Texans.

As for any anti-Semitism (which is what I presume you were hinting at) there seems to be very little. I have not seen any and many of the girls already know my religion****. I want them to know. Besides the kids from Martins Creek are swell and I know and I am sure would stick up for me if trouble arose–and I don't think this would ever happen. Don't worry!

The one thing I miss most besides a good cup of coffee and hot eggs for breakfast is a good glass of water. I don't think I'll ever get used to this water. You can actually taste the chlorine in it. The water here is very hard making it quite difficult to wash. So far, I have done most of my laundry because I sent it out once and it came back dirty so I'll keep my clothes dirty by washing them myself–at least as long as I can. Must go now.

Love to all,

Bernice.

p.s. We got paid last night and I had about $53 left when I got through. Will send some home when I see what my expenses will be this month.

* Conmar is the zipper manufacturer where I worked as private secretary to the patent attorney.

** The graduating class referred to was 44-2, Mar. 11, 1944.

*** Irv Shapiro was a platonic friend who sometimes signed his letters "Love, Brotherly (?) Irv."

****Interesting to note–in our bay of six, we practiced six different religions and all got along well. Baptist, Christian Science, Jewish, Mormon, Protestant, Seventh Day Adventist. It can be done.

## V-mail from Lloyd in England

March 14, 1944

Dear Bernice,

Boy, that address of yours is a killer. Why don't you put your bed number on it? Well, at last the mail is beginning to come through. For the past couple of days several letters have arrived from Elea, one from Sol, one from Paul, and today one from Mom. Yours haven't decided to bless me with their appearance but Texas you know is a long way off. Mom tells me you are pretty busy so don't feel bad if you don't have time to write often. I'll understand.

Life here has been very interesting and at times very dull. The only form of entertainment has been an occasional movie and a couple of visits to hear the London Philharmonic. Scheherazade–one of the concerts–very nice and also a change. Have really been working and putting in the hours of late, hope I get something out of it, if you know what I mean.

Mom has not written me much about just what you are doing way down there in Texas but I know a letter from you will give me all the dope, so patient I'll be. She had a call from Connie* who was changing trains in New York City, on her way back to Kalamazoo to visit her fiancé, who is now out of the Army due to a broken back. Don't know the details since I haven't heard from Connie for a good five months.

Well my winged sister, I sincerely hope that everything is working out OK and that things are not getting too tough. Just remember that it will be worth it in the end and that I know you can do most anything you set out to do.

Good luck and lots of love,

Lloyd

* Connie Arkind is our first cousin. She was in the Marines.

# PRIMARY PHASE OF TRAINING

**We began flying February 28, 1944.**

March 14, 1944

Dear Mom,

I just said to myself as I trotted back from the flight line, "I shall write my dear sweet mother a letter," and so here it is. Rather nice to be able to say that and then have the time to do it. The reason we have time is that we were just released from the flight line two hours early, after another day of no flying due to the wind. It is either wind or rain.

The new class arrived yesterday containing Kay Gladding* and Katie Leeds*. We of W-7 are thrilled no end to have W-8 with us because that means we are no longer the babies of the post. Consequently, we have been strutting around with our chests well inflated. We visited the new class last night in their bay areas and sang them songs and helped them with their beds and stuff and tried in general to make their first evening as pleasant and home-like as possible. This was done for us and we sure appreciated it.

The laundry situation here is just awful. We have tried a couple of laundry women, maids who clean around the post, and they are awful. The regular laundry is just as bad. None of them get the clothes clean. I have been endeavoring to do my own wash but the water is so hard even I have difficulty getting the stuff clean. I think I shall reach the happy medium of washing all my things except the towels**.

I would love to take pictures but I have no film. It would be swell if you could get some but I guess you are having as much trouble as I am getting it.

How is the engagement announcement coming along? I wrote Elea and Lloyd congratulating them***.

The graduation**** Friday with about nine of the biggest generals in the Air Force was a great success. We marched in a parade and everyone on the post had her fingers crossed. You see, we take our drillmaster as a joke and the guys at the head of our drilling were just sure we would do a sloppy job or be out of step or something. But we fooled them and it was really nice*****.

Saturday night I went into town for the first time since I came here. The reason I went was that Marie Lynch and another girl gave a dinner party at one of the local restaurants for their birthdays. It was very nice. We have started a custom of buying the girls from Martins Creek a Fifinella pin when they have a birthday. We make a big fuss over them and make them feel good.

We are having a final exam in theory of flight this week. I just never have time to study. Let me know how Jackie is getting along. Is she going to bed early? Take care of yourself Mommy dear.

Love,
Bernice

* They were both from Martins Creek.
** Many of us discovered that the best way to wash our zoot suits was to wear them in the shower, soap them, then rinse them off and hang them outside our bays to dry.
*** They wanted to become engaged while Lloyd was still overseas. The two families arranged a date, had a party and my mother acted in Lloyd's behalf by presenting Elea with the diamond engagement ring.
**** Referring to Class 44-2 graduation.
***** Other than regular marching, we had been taught some Marine drill marching that we were practicing. At the proper time the drill 'sergeant' would call out "To the Four Winds–MARCH." Upon hearing the word MARCH, each person would leave the regular formation and start counting to herself, going out a certain number of steps, changing direction, and eventually falling back into regular formation. Anyone who has seen the Marines do this type of marching will understand how impressive it is. You can see why Lieutenant La Rue was nervous because one person missing a count can ruin the entire formation.

*March 11, 1944–Graduation class of 44-2. Nine generals attended including General "Hap" Arnold. He presented the Air Medal to Barbara Erickson (London) for outstanding work in the Ferry Command.*

*Our marching prowess–these are the uniforms that the WASP trainees wore for formal occasions prior to being issued the Santiago blue uniforms at graduation.*

POSTCARD
March 15, 1944

Dear Mom,

Just a couple of minutes before mess–I just wanted to let you know I soloed today. I now have nine hours and thirty-two minutes. Gee it was swell. Now I'll really have to get on the ball and work real hard.

Love to all,
Bernice

March 16, 1944

Dear Mom,

Thought you would enjoy seeing a picture of the ship I fly. It is really a wonderful plane.

I got your letter about Janette today. I heard the news the day after it happened in a telegram from Chris* addressed to Gen. I took the news OK but needless to say was very sad and quiet for a few days. Betty was correct in sending me the details because not knowing how it happened was bothering us all. The thing that really had me concerned was that you would hear the news and worry. Now that I see how you feel and are taking it I feel much better. It was swell of you to go to the funeral and the Yoder's home.

You are the most thoughtful mother in the world. Please, Mom, don't ever worry. This accident has taught me you can never be too careful and to be on the job every second. We also found out that the country around Jefferson City, Missouri, is the most treacherous in America. If you're careful, things like that don't happen so your little daughter is quite safe. I have so much to tell you that I'll have to continue in another letter.

Much love to all,

Bernice

*Chris Stohlfus owned a Waco 125-horsepower open cockpit aircraft, which he kept at Fogelsville, Pennsylvania. The month prior to entering WASP training, a few of us went there to fly in that higher horsepower aircraft. It was there that we met Janette Yoder, 22. Robert Snelling, 21, a friend of hers was flying her to Sweetwater to enter WASP training. En route, they landed at Rolla, Missouri, only to find it was an abandoned airport. They took the chance of having enough fuel to reach Springfield. Fourteen miles from their destination they unsuccessfully attempted a forced landing in a field and crashed, killing them both. Inspectors from the Civil Aeronautics Administration found the plane structurally perfect—there just wasn't a drop of gasoline in the tank. This was determined pilot error.


NOTE: Avenger Field was used for practice by the BT-13 and AT-6 aircraft which had radios. The Stearman aircraft used auxiliary fields a distance from Avenger Field. The first Stearman student of the day would leave Avenger, do her hour of practice and then land at an auxiliary field. The rest of the students were transported to the auxiliary field in a vehicle we dubbed the 'cattle car'. The last student of the day after her practice would then bring the ship back to Avenger Field. The Stearman had no radio. Landing among all the aircraft that had radios was stressful and dangerous. There were mid-air collisions resulting in deaths at Avenger Field and elsewhere. Instructors always told students to keep their heads on a swivel. At Avenger, the student would enter the traffic pattern, look to the tower for a green light, which gave her permission to land. If she received a red light she would have to continue flying the pattern until given a green.

*Bee at the auxiliary field wearing some winter gear. We also had fleece lined helmet and pants. Note adhesive tape on pants leg. We would make notes on this tape.*

*Bee ready to get into Stearman with parachute. We always flew with a parachute.*

*We called the bus used to transport us to the auxiliary field 'cattle car'.*

*Printed on bottom of Postcard*
KEEP 'EM FLYING IN COMBAT TEAMS
THE ENEMY IS LISTENING—DON'T SAY IT
THE ENEMY CAN READ—DON'T WRITE IT

*Bill "Alfafa" Murray my first instructor whom I had until March 15th since he was a check pilot. If a student was not doing well, she was put up for a check ride. Also, when finishing a phase of training, you had to pass a civilian and army check ride.*

*Bernice and D. H. "Mac" McLandress, my second Stearman instructor*

38

Dear Mom,

I'm sorry I ever wrote you about my laundry. It is not as bad as I portrayed it I am sure. Wrapping it to mail and all of that would be more bother than just using dirty stuff or letting it rot, or washing it myself, or what have you, so please don't give it another thought. Also no extra sets of anything by any means because first, I have more than ample and second, I have no room in my locker for another thing and I would only have to store it in my suitcase which means I would never get to use it anyway.

Thanks loads for sending me more tea. This will be plenty for a while and if I need more I'll ask for it and not be shy. You see we can only get loose tea in town, which is a nuisance because then the kids have to bring strainers to supper with them. All I do is stick a tea ball in my pocket and go. I have a nice supply now.

Thanks ever so much for handling my income tax so well. The amount of the check was $73.75–right? Just to keep the records straight between you and me here is what my checkbook looks like:

Deposited  $290.10            Checks
            -230.15         $132.40 flying
                             14.00 dentist
                             73.75 income tax
                             10.00
                            $230.15

    Balance $59.95

About my pay—I don't know how it works but this is what I got. No one else knows how it works either.

Received net after income tax deductions:

$86.98 (it was not a whole month)        $86.98

Gym shoes and socks $ 3.55
Room and Board      29.70                -33.25
                   $33.25                $53.73

Cold cash received                       $53.73

Then there's $2 a month student fund and a small cleaning bill.

We sent the Yoders flowers and that was $2.00. Some of the kids had birthdays and with chipping in and all, that's another $5 or so, and so it goes. I think I'll keep the cash I have here now with me in case something else turns up. In a week or so I'll send home $30 or $35. I have enough cash on hand so don't worry.

How are you doing in school, Jake? I know you are taking good care of Mom and the house otherwise she would not have time to write me the nice long letters I have been getting so often.

About a gift from Irv–I finally thought of something I really want but would not get for myself–that is a good pair of sunglasses. I already wrote him that was what I wanted if he could get them. I won't wait until graduation, although I thought of telling him this, because he is determined to give me a gift now. Not only that but the same problem will arise at that time.

We definitely know we will soon be in the Army Air Force. Just what day the ax will fall is unknown to us, but we have been told that we will have the course lengthened three weeks, and we have been getting more drill and more military training as we go along. They have made a proviso (so I understand) that if you washout even under the Army, you have a choice of going back to civilian life or staying in the Air Force as a second lieutenant. I would choose the latter–this would be good at 2nd looie's pay. I think we will have fewer expenses if we are in the Army than we have now. In the end I am sure it would be better.

I am glad Best & Co. broke their little hearts and gave you a raise. You deserve it only ten times or so more.

As long as you are going to present the ring*1 know it will be done well and will hold just as much sentiment as if Lloyd were doing it only not the same.
Lovingly,<br>Bernice

*Refers to the engagement of Elea and Lloyd performed by proxy.

V-mail from Lloyd in England

March 19, 1944

Dear Bernice,

Yesterday I received a package from Elea with olives, candy and writing paper. I use v-mail on you. I think it is quicker in the long run. And as I have said before, don't worry if you do not have time to write to me often, I understand well enough. It is more important to write to Mom because I know that she will worry if you do not. I know how it is going to an Army or similar school. You have, or think you have time but you are damned if you can find out where it goes.

Your schedule sounds rather on the "G.I." side and I can appreciate it. But I also know that you will be the better off for it. Sleeping good and all that. You know the old story. Since your letter is a month old, I hope that you have been able to start your flight training because I know that is your chief interest and the reason that you are in Texas in the first place. I'll probably be re-echoing Mom if I say to take care of yourself and be as careful as possible. But I guess I need not go into all that. I think you realize what it is all about. Don't forget, too, that you have a wedding to attend. And while I'm on that subject (I usually do get around to it at some time or other) you don't know how happy you made me feel when I read in your letters that you think a lot of Elea. It really does. And don't ever think that it is none of your business. Yes, Elea and I are going to announce our engagement. Since the mail situation is pretty bad lately (by the way, note the new address), who knows? I may already be engaged, formally that is since Elea and I had made up our minds, even before I left the States. If we had had time before I left, we probably would have married then. But things moved too quickly and too uncertainly. I never knew from one day to the next back in November whether or not I would be home on the following day. No way to spend a honeymoon, I assure you. And time spent apart does not seem to have effected our affections, which indicates that the future (whatever that is) will be a happy one.

You know you are very swell. And for a sister, I don't think that I could have better.

Well so long and keep 'em flying.
                    Love,
                            Lloyd


                                                        March 20, 1944
Dear Mom,

I am starting this five minutes before taps and so know I shall not finish it tonight. I flew two and a half hours today and boy am I tired. One hour and forty minutes was solo on takeoffs and landings. You see we must have three supervised solos before we can take a ship up by ourselves and fly away from the field to practice air work. A supervised solo is when the instructor sits on the ground and watches everything you do and all your landings and when you come down he runs over and bawls you out and then sends you up again.

Golly, Mr. Murray is swell and he sure goes through a lot with dopey me as a student. He really is the best instructor on the field and I am the envy of the whole class. I now have fourteen and a half hours. Tomorrow I go off by myself for one and a half hours and have dual for one hour. The wash-outs are beginning to happen and it is very depressing and unhappy for all concerned. It really scares me. I love it so and become more and more enthused with flying every day that if anything ever happens I think I'll die. I try very hard not to think of this but it is always in the back of everyone's mind.

Next a.m.–we just got a bit of good news. We are supposed to have PT right after breakfast but it was called off today. This gives us a whole hour to ourselves. I guess I'll do some studying when I finish this. An hour here is a piece of luxury.

Our schedule this week is not too bad;

> 6:50–breakfast–we can sleep until about 6:30
> 7:40–PT–we must have our beds made and bays clean
> before we leave.
> 8:55–12:00 ground school
> 12:05–mess
> 12:55–flight line
> 7:15–mess–I am usually still on flight line.

Then we have the evening to study, wash, shower, etc. and before you can turn around taps have blown. I am never sorry because it is a very tiring day but one filled with lots of laughs.

Believe it or not, you never get a chance to read your mail when it is handed out because there is always something going on. And boy oh boy the letters really burn a hole in your pocket while you wait for a chance to read them.

I have been getting letters from Mr. Rabinow* (Conmar does, not know, of course) and he says Mr. Konoff** just returned from a vacation and is raising the roof in his usual style. I also hear quite frequently from Sol Winick, the boy I worked with, who is stationed at Camp Hood, Texas.

Much love,
Bernice

* Mr. Rabinow was the head of the Engineering Department for Conmar where I had worked. There had never been women in that department. He wanted to see if a woman working there would disrupt things. For a while I spent half a day in his department being instructed in engineering drafting. After I left, they did hire some women.
** Mr. Konoff was the owner of the company.

March 23, 1944 letter from my mother, "Betty read in today's paper that the army expects to take it over."

March 27, 1944

Dear Mom,

Saturday and Sunday mornings are supposed to be our free time—we had to take some more tests for the Army Air Force, similar to the ones we took before. Tomorrow we have to undergo the physical part of the tests. These are experimental and will not fail us if we don't pass. They need statistics to see how they can use the tests for future women applicants.

I was sure glad to hear that Betty has her application. It really won't be too bad being in the Army. We live now just as strictly as if we were in. The part that irks us more about these tests is that they were all done on our free time and we had no chance to go to town or sleep or write at all this week.

I sure wish I could get some film so I could take some snaps. Any chance of you getting some 620s?

By the way, I passed my first check ride. However, I lost Mr. Murray. It was inevitable since he got busy with check rides. Now I have a Mr. McLandress. He is nice but not nearly as good as Murray. I would give anything to have Murray but it is impossible. Anyway he promised to give me my check, which I am sure will end up in a valuable lesson.

Love to Dad and Jackie and a great big fat kiss for you.
Love,<br>Deine Dotter

p.s. In reply to my letter to Elea, she suggested I get her an album of *Porgy and Bess*. She noted that records would be nice instead of lingerie or something so personal because this way Lloyd too can enjoy the gift. Isn't that a sweet thought and so like Elea.

Guess what the latest is with the show? They liked it so much that we now have to put it on for Camp Tye–an Air Force Base. We are flattered but weary as the devil, and a trifle annoyed at having to spend so much of our spare time with the show that was just put on for the amusement of Avenger Field.

NOTE: We were bussed to Camp Barkeley March 17th to give our show. Since there was no stage entrance, we fifteen girl student flyers had to march in from the front door and walk down the center aisle through this already seated enthusiastic crowd of whistling and hooting young men. We could do nothing wrong! They loved us! A few days later Mrs. Deaton called us to a meeting. Our show was such a success she wanted to know if we would like to 'take it on the road'. When we asked what would happen with our flight training if we said yes, we were told we would have to give that up.

**There wasn't a yes in the crowd!**

*In front of our barracks Gerry Ashwell\*, Marie Lynch, Alice Gartland, Winnie Lo Pinto, Bee Falk\* Five of the six of us who learned to fly at Martins Creek, Pennsylvania and who came together for 44-7 class.*
*\*Graduated–including Betty Pettitt not shown here.*

*Bee reading one of those coveted letters from home to Alice Gartland.*

44

April 5, 1944

Dear Mom,

Things have been happening fast and furiously around here–so fast I have not had a minute to write.

First of all and the saddest is that Marie Lynch, Winnie Lo Pinto, Grace McElligott and Alice Gartland all failed check rides today. This means they get two more check rides, one civilian and one Army. If they fail these, they are out. This is very depressing indeed. Alice has been in a slump for the past five days, and when you lose the confidence in yourself that is so important in flying, you just do a lousy job no matter how hard you try. I know because that is what happened to me before I ever soloed at Martins Creek, remember? That question you used to ask me every weekend and always got the same dejected reply.* This is the same thing only with a few more hours under her belt. We all know Alice can do it if she could only have time to get out of her slump but the program here has no time to wait for people to get out of slumps. We have been spending every spare moment possible with Alice trying to get her perked up trying everything we know but it all seems to have been useless. I just hope she snaps out of it before tomorrow.

The program has been getting more and more difficult as time goes on and they expect a lot from us. I am having my troubles right now with lazy eights, chandelles, stalls and lots of other things.** Work at it is all I can do and if just trying would get me there I would already have my silver wings.

Gee, Mom, thanks loads for the package with the razors, tea balls, bras and M&M's. I liked the note in the M&M's the best. If you only knew how fitting it is because my pockets are always stuffed with something to eat on the flight line. I offered everyone some M&M's and showed them all the note. Mr. Murray, my ex-instructor, grinned from ear to ear when he read it and I could tell he thought it was cute.***

Thanks too for the bras. I really don't need anything. I am trying to keep my things down to as few as possible because we don't have much room.

By the way, I discovered ants in my locker tonight. I think it was because of a donut I put there this afternoon. Taps are about to blow in two minutes so I'll sign off because I do want you to get some word from me this week.

G'nite now,

Much love,

Bernice

* I was referring to the first time I had soloed at Martins Creek. I had twenty-three hours of dual before 1 soloed on August 1, 1943.

** Various maneuvers, some almost aerobatic, to teach you to control the aircraft.

*** They all enjoyed that my mother thought of sending M&M's for my pocket, which is where they went. We had large pockets in the legs of our zoot suits. I would stash fruit and goodies, which I shared on the flight line. The M&M's were perfect!

April 11, 1944

Dear Mom,

Just time for a short one. Most importantly, I don't ever want to hear of you writing things like, *Hope I don't annoy you too much with too much in one letter.* I eat up every word you write. If you wrote a book every time, it still would not be enough.

Glad to hear the party was such a success. I sure wish I could have been there. I'm glad you gave Elea a watch.

By the way, I have my Army progress check ride tomorrow. I hope I pass.

Marie Lynch and Winnie Lo Pinto have washed-out. Grace McEllicott is on her way and Alice Gartland is having trouble. I feel terrible about the whole thing–and fearful. Anyway, no one can say I'm not trying. We have already lost a good percentage of our class.

Much love,
Bernice

April 13, 1944

Dear Mom,

At this point, we are having a sixty-mile an hour wind carrying with it all the sand in Texas. Boy, it really is blowing and your eyes and nose and mouth are just filled with sand all the time.

Some sad news–Alice washed-out and so did Marie, Winnie and Grace. They have eliminated quite a few of our class. Yesterday I took my Army check ride and passed–hallelujah! Now I have just one more civilian check and if I pass, I will be all set for the next part of the training. We may get a three-day pass between. I hope so. Just to have a chance to sleep and eat from plates instead of tin trays will be good.

I hope, I hope, I hope, I pass my last check. About chandelles and lazy eights, I will have to explain them when I see you because it would be impossible for me to describe in words on paper. They are exercises in the plane. We have started acrobatics and they sure are fun–except I can't do them too well. I get upside down and have a little trouble getting around again much to the delight of Mr. McLandress (my instructor).

Have to go to gym now so I'll sign off.

Much love,

Bernice

NOTE: Alice Gartland, Marie Lynch, Winnie Lo Pinto, Grace McElligott were all from Martins Creek, where so many of us learned to fly. They started flying in Sweetwater on February 28th, and after a month and five days of flying, they washed-out. About washing-out, this was something we all feared. The fact that one could not succeed was depressing and weighed on all our minds throughout the entire program. It was not as if everyone who applied could have been successful, it was that you had to learn and be able to do so much in such a short period of time. There were also some personality clashes between student and instructor. We were told prior to commencing flying that if we felt there might be difficulty with an instructor, it would not be held against us if we requested a different instructor. Some did not take this advice and the consequences were often washing-out.


### V-mail from Lloyd

April 19, 1944

Dear Bernice,

Thanks for all the compliments about Elea (and me). I'm very glad that you feel the way you do about her. It certainly makes me feel better and also more confident. It looks like I should have made up my mind sooner. I guess though that it had been made up but it took a while for things to happen so that the outside world could catch on. Actually had I had a little more time in November while I was in New York I would probably have been married by now. But things happened so quickly that there wasn't time, never knowing from one day to the next whether or not you could be able to go home was quite a strain to say the least. But those four 'evenings' were the final turning point. We both had been a little doubtful about things, just how we stood, until then. Somehow something happened that flipped the coin to the sure thing side. Do I talk a little out of my head or does it make sense to you, oh great wise sister?

With all my excuses about working hard you will probably find it rather difficult to reconcile the fact that last week I saw two concerts, one musical play and a ballet. Of course, it meant staying up for twenty-four hours at a stretch to do it but I guess the change of atmosphere was worth it. The concerts were OK, the first, that is, they played some Brahms and Beethoven. The second would have been OK too, Bach, if the orchestra had been good. But, confidentially... The musical was called The Dancing Years and was very good. It should have been since it has been playing in London for about four or five years. Before the war even. The ballet, well, it wasn't bad, or too good. It was a young company. They were not very polished but I guess a few more years will give them that. It was not as good as the Russian Ballet that I saw when I lived in Trenton.

Good luck, Kiddo, and thanks again. What for? Your understanding.

Love,
Lloyd


April 24, 1944

Dear Mom,

First let me say what a very happy kid I am. I passed my Army check, I passed my final civilian check and I finished my seventy hours in the Stearman PT-17–that means I have finished primary. Happy Day! The first milestone has been passed. Some of the kids still have some time to make up so I have this a.m. free to try to get rid of that stack of twenty letters piled up at my right. We should start in the AT-6 tomorrow and as soon as I get postcards with their pictures, I shall send you one.

Friday I finished flying, so Saturday Betty Pettitt who is also finished, another girl and I got special passes to go to a nearby lake. We bought stuff for a picnic lunch and incidentally the hard boiled eggs Jackie and you sent made the picnic lunch a real one. We were all set to go when a dust storm came up. We knew it would not be nice at the lake so we took our lunch and went to the USO in town and in the privacy of a very nice and quiet ladies lounge ate our picnic lunch. Then we wandered around the USO, spoke to some soldiers, played Ping-Pong, listened to some records, then went out to eat and came back to the post.

Sunday we once again gathered up a picnic lunch and went to the lake, this time with the fellows. We had a marvelous time. It is really a beautiful spot with lots and lots of trees. You have no idea just how much a tree means to you until you have none–"a poem as lovely as a tree." At camp we haven't any trees at all and, boy, is it hot in the summer. So far we still have had rather cool weather with just a day here and there that is hot. There seems to be no spring at all in Texas. At least you can't smell it.

What are you trying to do to me? Kill me? That description of the dinner sent me practically into a case of wild hysteria. What I wouldn't give for a nice baked dinner. You know these southerners have an idea they must disguise all foods. Our string beans and vegetables are cooked with either ham bones or bacon. Spare ribs and pork chops, both greasy, make up most of our meat dishes. We have lots of mashed potatoes. The one thing that annoys me more than anything is the starchy menu–also, the lack of fresh vegetables. It really isn't too bad as a whole just poorly planned.

Thanks for praying for me, Mom, I really need it. Remember, food is forbidden in the bays so we have to hide it as best we can. I'm eating some of the candy you sent me now. I have been eating too much candy lately. Better go to the dentist. By the way, what you wrote with the M&M's was that they were for me to put in my pocket for the flight line.

Thanks for the clippings. Julian* is a real hero.

Much love,
Deine Tochter

* Julian Reichman, a friend in the Infantry in Europe. He was with the Bomb Demolition Squad–detonating live bombs and he lost some of his hearing.

April 24, 1944

Dear Jackie,

My flying, as you have read in my other letters, is creeping along. So far I have not received any demerits but this cannot last very long. Soon I will do something wrong or not clean my locker right or make my bed improperly and so will receive demerits.

Goodbye for now Big Sister and keep up the good work–study hard too, so you can be a smart kid.

Lots of love from Your Little Sister,
B

NOTE: The last hour of dual in the Stearman was considered a 'buddy ride,' that is, the student would fly from the front seat where the instructor usually sat and act as the 'instructor.' The instructor would fly in the back seat acting as the 'student' and had to do what the 'instructor' told him. I had planned that when we got to the altitude for doing acrobatics, I would do a loop, at the top of which I would tell him, "You've Got It!!!" To make matters more interesting, I gave him my helmet (too small for him) and I wore his (too large for me).

Since there was no radio, we communicated through a gosport. The instructor speaks through a funnel-like contraption that has a hose that connects into the student's helmet by each ear. In other words, the student cannot speak to the instructor in the air. We reached the proper altitude for doing acrobatics and I performed the loop except at the top of the loop the too big helmet fell over my eyes and the gosport flew from my hands. The airplane did not complete the loop but I managed to shout, "You've got it!!!" We both had a good laugh when we reached the safety of the ground

*Instructor McLandress getting ready for 'buddy ride.'*

*Bee eating an apple before the 'buddy ride'*

## NEXT PHASE OF TRAINING

April 30, 1944

Dear Mom,

We don't know from one day to the next whether we will be getting in the Army and have uniforms or whether we will be kicked out entirely. I fear the latter. Perhaps a letter from you and some of our friends like Sam, Amelia and those guys to our congressman urging him to vote the WASP into the Army Air Force would help. You might say that men are needed in other branches of service, such as the Infantry, where women are absolutely useless so why not let the men go into the Infantry and permit the women to do a job that already has been proven they can do and can do well. Besides, most of the instructors who are squawking could have gotten a commission in the Air Force months ago but many of them being draft and duty dodgers preferred to stay in the reserve. Now when they know they will be put in the Infantry or some other branch of service they are fighting to get in the Air Force. They shirked their duties first and now they must pay for it. By the way, if you write don't mention you have a daughter in the WASP.

Sorry to have gone so far astray and so vehemently but we are rather griped about the whole situation down here.

Now for the AT-6–what a beautiful airplane–650 horsepower purring along and just full of gadgets. The cockpit procedure is very long and difficult. We use radios in this ship. Every time we takeoff or land we have to call the tower for permission. So far I have only two hours–weather being bad again. Somehow I can't imagine soloing that airplane in from eight to twelve hours.

Even the instructors say that it is a big jump from a PT-17 with 220-horsepower to an AT-6. The cadets don't even have that big a jump.*

Some time I'll tell you everything you are doing on takeoffs and landings besides flying the airplane–what a mess–but I love it.

We also start Link training. When we do not fly, we have Link. This is a make-believe airplane into which you close yourself–like closing yourself into a black box. In front of you glow many illuminated instruments. The Link trainer simulates the cockpit of an airplane. It's up to you to fly the ship by instruments only. As soon as we finish in the AT-6 we are supposed to go into instrument flying and Link is an aid to that. It is enough to drive you daffy trying to watch all the gadgets at once. We started meteorology in ground school and are still taking navigation and engine maintenance.

Much love to all and thanks again Mommy dear,
Deine daughter

p.s. I got a special shoe stamp** because I need another pair of brown shoes. Do you suppose you could get me another pair of the 'military dress' shoes like the ones I got in Best's? They are so comfortable and I believe will be regulation shoes if we get in the Army. They are easier than laced shoes to keep polished. If you can't get them, send the stamp back and I'll get a pair in town. Please do not get me others because you know my feet and I might have to try them on.

*Training had traditionally been from a primary trainer to a basic trainer to an advanced trainer. The class of 44-4 (three classes ahead of us) was the first class of trainees to go directly into the AT-6 advanced trainer from the PT-17 primary trainer. Jacqueline Cochran visited Sweetwater to explain that this was the first time the Air Force was taking this step and if it proved successful the male cadets would be trained in this manner.

We were the guinea pigs!

** Because of shortages during the war civilians were issued stamps to allow them to buy shoes, meat, gasoline, sugar, etc.

NOTE: The Link trainer was for practicing flying on instruments only. The door and hood are closed leaving the student in the dark except for the lighted instruments and her navigation paper work. She then practices flying without visual contact with the ground. The instructor has a desk outside the trainer where he follows her flight, which is projected on paper with a stylus. Today more sophisticated simulators are used.

*Bee having a serious conversation with her AT-6 instructor, Les L. Jones. His nickname was "Stinky" because one time he made a forced landing in a septic field. I started AT-6 training April 27th and soloed after ten and a half hours of dual.*

*Sitting on wing of AT-6. The tower in the background.*

# Letter from Lloyd

May 2, 1944

Dear Bernice,

    I don't believe I ever told you about my visit to New Gardens. This is a really beautiful place to see and is a real must on anyone's list who comes to England in the spring or summer. Now it is particularly decorative since both cherry trees and magnolia trees are in full flower. Then there are hundreds of flower-beds with all sorts of flowers. There are also greenhouses with tropical plants like orchids and palm trees and cacti and such. You can spend hours in the place always seeing something new. I still haven't seen all of it and will probably try to visit it again sometime.

    Damn I wish this war were over.

All for now, Kiddo. How's with the flying?

Love,<br>Lloyd

Monday May 8, 1944

Dear Mom,

    We had a lovely day yesterday. We all went to Sweetwater Lake, which is about a twenty-minute bus ride from here, and is a very lovely spot. We made a picnic lunch in the camp kitchen, which was really nice. They gave us tomatoes and everything. We went swimming. The weather was stifling and the water was ice cold. It sure felt good though. We had a really nice time. 'We' are about fifteen girls from our class.

    I am still struggling with the AT-6. It does not come easily to me. You know, it really is a big ship with ever so much to do all at once. That is all I can say about my flying at present, except that I have six and a half hours so far in the AT-6. Link training continues and this is real torture. We are closed up in the dark for an hour or more at a time. And all the gadgets...

    About ground school–we started code today and it really is going to be something. We will have to be able to do eight words a minute. We finished engines on Saturday and are now taking code, instruments and meteorology. We also finished basic navigation and shall take advanced later on.

*I enclosed this picture:*

In case you are interested, I am enclosing other proofs for you to look at. Please return them when you are thru. I think I took the best choice to be made up but let me know what you think. The pigtail ones are some the photographer took on his own. He said he did it because he liked my pigtails so well and just wanted to take some shots.

Needless to say, Mom, I sure wish I could be home to help the best Mom in the world celebrate Mother's Day. But maybe next year you will have both of your older children home to do just that. Goodbye for now, Honey, and thank you for being such a wonderful mother.

Love, hugs and kisses,<br>
Bernice

May 11, 1944

Dearest Mom,

With the help of prayers from myself and my five bay mates two nights in a row I managed to at long last solo the AT-6 today. Golly, Mom, it sure is hard work to fly this plane. I am going to have to work very hard to get through this phase but if hard work will do it, you can be assured I will make it, Mom. This is a picture of the ship. I wish I could take a snap shot of me next to it but we are not allowed to do so. By the way I did receive the two films and thanks loads, Honey.

Again,

Happy Mother's Day.

Much love, Bernice

A. T. 6

May 16, 1944

Dear Ma,

Your daughter gets more and more tired as time goes by. Let me tell you of my schedule yesterday. Arose at 6:30 a.m., breakfast–6:45, gym–7:20, recall from gym–8:20, ground school from–9:00 to 12:00, lunch–12:25, flight line–1:25, recall from flight line, for me anyway–8:30 p.m. Mess hall closes at 8:30 and I had to go in the kitchen and practically beg for some food. At 9:00 I had Link for one hour and to bed at 10:00. One thing that takes up so much time is the changing of clothes in between everything you do around here.*

By the way, I passed my civilian check in the AT-6 yesterday. My flying is still extremely shaky and I know I shall just have to hope, pray and worry my way through this phase.

Studies are piling up and we are given outside studying to do but as you can see we have no time for study. My ground school marks have been pretty good all along anyway so I won't have to worry much about that.

Love,
Bernice

* On the flight line, we wore zoot suits. For gym we changed to gym

clothes. For ground school we changed to more formal dress, white shirts and officer's pinks (slacks).

May 22, 1944

Dear Mom,

First of all I'll give you the best news. I finished the AT-6 and passed both my check rides. I might add that I just passed my Army check ride but the important part is that I did pass. We have various jobs to do around the post and have to prepare for, and stay for graduation* tomorrow morning. Then we have a pass until Thursday night and then Friday we start instrument flying and continue with Link.

Some of the kids and I are going by bus to San Angelo which is only two hours from here. We are going mainly for lots of sleep because we are all really worn out. Everyone has been getting on everyone else's nerves lately. Then too, Sweetwater is a dry town and we are looking forward to a good cold glass of beer and some fresh shrimp in San Angelo.

I had a lovely day yesterday. This boy from Barkeley whose name is Bert Swensen came out here and we went to a movie Saturday night and Sunday we went to lunch, then horse back riding, then swimming, then dinner and then dashed back to camp just in time.

By the way, Mom, you sure would like all the flowers here. Fields and fields of beautiful wild flowers some I have never seen before. And the cacti are now in bloom. They have yellow and rose blooms about the size of a rose and with many petals. They do look a lot like roses but not as full and their petals look as if they have been waxed. They really look like artificial flowers. They are beautiful and look slightly ridiculous on those cactus plants.

We got a two-day pass and we all packed up in a hurry and dashed to San Angelo. We had a marvelous time, staying at a hotel that was very lovely, carpets, soft beds, a big bathtub and lots of privacy. We didn't do much except eat, sleep, shop and spend money.

Taps have blown, Mom, so I'll have to dash.

Much love, Honey,

Bernice

By the way, Alice Gartland is in California and I asked her to let me know what living conditions are out there. She has written me and says as far as Los Angeles is concerned it is impossible right now. She looked around in papers and stuff, and even asked her aunt's landlord if he had a place, and what the possibilities were. It seems there are no possibilities and housing conditions are quite desperate. Thought you would be interested.

Bed check has been around, so I sneaked into the john and closed the door to finish this letter. We have been having blisteringly hot weather and it is only May. Can you imagine what July and August will be like?

Gosh I'm tired.

G'nite again. .

* The graduation was that of Class 44-4.

*Jacqueline Cochran, Ethel Sheehy, Maj. Gen. Jacob B. Fickle, Acting Commander AAF Training Command presenting diploma to graduating WASP. Background: Mrs. Robert D. Patterson, wife of Under Secretary of War.*

NOTE: The thermometer often reached 100 degrees as early as April and stayed there or higher for five months.

# SIX

# INSTRUMENT TRAINING

May 26, 1944

Dear Mom,

We were pre-flighted* on instruments and start flying tomorrow. This is really a tough phase. Gotta run now.

Much love,

Bernice

*Explanation of pre-flighted in letter of June 6.

## V-mail from Lloyd in England

May 25, 1944

Dear Bernice,

I still think you should disown me for a brother. To say I neglect writing is criminal. But–how's the flying? You must be past the halfway mark by now. Let's keep the fingers crossed.

Saw a play and movie in London this week with the captain in charge of my section. The play *Blithe Spirit* was an excellent comedy. All about a man who has married after his first wife died rather young. Through the influence of a medium his first wife is able to come back to haunt him. She is a very gay and mischievous person and causes quite a commotion–especially since she is only visible and audible to him (and the audience). Remarks, which he addresses to the ghost, are misinterpreted by his wife. All gets very complicated especially when his second wife comes back as a spirit after she gets killed in an automobile accident through the influence of his first wife. She meant to kill her husband so she could have his company

in the spirit world. Then the spirits find that they cannot get back to the spirit world. They try everything–séance–magic–finally they do get away because the maid is psychic or something, which leaves the husband free and carefree. This doesn't displease him. He's glad to get rid of both of them. The movie I saw was *Ferry by Gaslight*, also very good.
Gotta go now.

Good luck,
Love, Lloyd

In a June 2, 1944 letter from my mother, she wrote: "Am enclosing an article about Jacqueline Cochran becoming a Colonel and the Air Corps taking over. I'm glad that's settled."

May 30, 1944

Dear Mom,

These are the planes we are flying now. We sit in the back seat with a hood over us. We cannot see out and have to fly by instruments and radio. We just started. It is very difficult and necessitates lots of study but is very interesting.

By the way, if you can get more bras would you get three or four size 34, and two size 36 (B cup)–preferably white. The girls are having a devil of a time getting them here.

We start ground school at 7:00 in the morning and go straight through the day with school and flying ending the day with night classes in the Link. Taps will soon blow–I'll have to dash. We are having an instrument test tomorrow a.m. and I haven't studied yet–oh me.

Much Love, Honey, and please take care of yourself,
Bernice

*BT-13 Two-placed single engine basic training aircraft.*

*Our Instrument Instructor, Kenneth "Doc" Morgan and his three students, Beverly Frisbie, Penny Halladay and Bee Falk*

*Bee, on the wing of the 450-horsepower fixed gear BT-13 in which we learned instrument flying.*

*This is a 'ready room' where instructors and students assembled to see the flight schedule for the day and receive instruction.*

# OUR PET DOGS

There were stray dogs around the base, which we 'adopted.'

*COWFACE–for obvious reasons.*

*VERTIGO–because he walked at an angle.*

*DOC–named for our instructor*

NOTE: We practiced instrument flying at the nearby Abilene radio range. When Bev Frisbie and I landed at Abilene Airport to change seats we saw a deserted puppy. We sneaked him into the BT-13 flew him back to Avenger Field and named him 'Doc' after our instrument instructor.

Dear Mom,

This is going to be a quickie. I am practically on the verge of a nervous breakdown. Instruments have turned from a course of interest to one of torture. It is without a doubt the most difficult task I have undertaken.

I am having lots of trouble and am working like a dog. It's no fun being cooped up under the hood for two and a half hours a day, concentrating so hard on your work that you come out with a headache. We are expected to study more than we have time for in order to pass the written instrument test.

By the way, I have passed my code and am able to take eight words a minute. We now have meteorology and instruments in ground school and will soon start on basic navigation. Until I finish instruments, or they finish me, I will not be writing to many people probably just you once a week.

I may have gained one or two pounds since I came here but no more. I fear I am losing weight on instruments. My appetite has become completely shot since beginning this phase. I'll be very happy when it's over.

Pre-flighted is the same as going into a new office or store where you are going to work and on the first day being shown all the procedures etc. We are shown the routine and introduced to the new airplane and its workings on the pre-flight without actually flying.

There are many cattle and sheep ranches in Texas, which explains why it is a wool center.

It still is not settled that we go in the Air Force although I wish it were. At least we have heard nothing definite.

Love to Dad and Jacki,
Bernice

* I didn't know at this writing that it was D-day.


## From Lloyd Referring to the D-day Invasion

June 9, 1944

Dear Bernice,

Just read the papers and I know it is stretching things a bit but imagine that I have been busy. Well, yes and no. Mostly both. But the thing is on its way–not a merry one by any means–and we settle back to the usual steady same old gait. It has been interesting seeing as much ahead of time as it is possible for a first lieutenant to see. *

Do you find that the going gets easier? Or don't they ever let up even after you have passed the first phases of training? Mom writes that you have had a couple of days off. I sure am glad to hear that. I know how a hot sun can wear you out. But I forgot–you are in the cool blue skies–dodging thunderstorms and line squalls–don't get too close.

Well, so long,
Lloyd.

* Lloyd was a meteorologist and had been working on determining the date for the D-day Invasion.

June 12, 1944

Dearest Mom,

Now that hot weather is coming upon us, we go swimming twice a week every other week, and once a week every other week during PT (physical training) classes.

About flying–I am still groaning and dreading instruments. It is such a relief when I can fly out from under the hood. Just being closed up like that is horrible. I am due for my first Army check any day now. Then we go on to radio flying (still under the hood and still instruments). You see there are radio ranges all over the country. Code sent out tells you what range you are on and by a very complicated method you figure out where you are on that range. All this time you are flying with no visual reference to the ground, and your ears are ringing from the signals constantly being sent over the earphones.

I hope I don't completely lose my mind before I finish instruments. There is really nothing new. The same busy, dizzy schedule and so it will be for some time.

I pray every night for Lloyd. Most of the girls down here who have fellows in the service have not heard from them in some time.

I hope you have been taking care of yourself. You have not mentioned your health lately. Please tell me how you are! Also really try to rest. I know it is hard but try. Gotta go now.

Lots of love,
Bernice

June 23, 1944

Dearest Folks,

The world once again looks rosy even if only for a few days. I have been a nervous wreck all week in anticipation of this final instrument radio check. Believe me this was the toughest I have ever been through (as I have so often said) and my physical health has felt it. I am extremely tired. Next week we will get two and a half days off and if possible will get a cabin at a nearby lake and just sleep and swim. The weather has been exceptionally hot and it is only June. Hotter days are to come!

Thank you so much for taking care of Father's Day for me. I was going to send a card but could not get off post to buy one and they did not have any here. I tried to send a telegram but they would not let me send one of that nature.

I have some very sad news. Gen North washed-out today. I think she got a raw deal. She got lost on a cross-country trip. She had two check rides and they said her flying was OK but she did not use her head enough. It doesn't seem fair that such a good pilot should be eliminated only a month before graduation. After all, navigation is supposed to teach you all the things about cross-country. The whole thing is just a shame.

About your coming down here–it really would be a lot better and faster for me to come home alone after graduation since I can probably get a ride–free–on a bomber going east. I could do this as a WASP but could not get one for you and Jackie because you are civilians. I would just have to take potluck myself. So you see if you can come in August it will be good. You understand that I will not be able to spend much time with you because we will be going on long cross-country trips and will never know when we will be away days at a time. If you could get here on a Friday, I could spend Saturday (half a day) and Sunday with you.

It will be very hot in August (it being beastly hot already) but I hope you don't mind too much. There is a local swimming pool and a movie for you and Jackie but I fear they are the only amusements offered. Anyway, I know you'll get a kick out of seeing the field and our life here. After all, generals and big shots come from miles around to see us. So my big shot Mom can tell them all she too saw Avenger Field. *

Here I come again with another favor. I will be needing my brown overnight bag (never mind the condition because it's going to get damaged in the plane anyway) for cross-country trips. When you send it, would you also enclose my blue sharkskin evening gown, the one with the buttons and the cape that was such a bargain a couple of years ago. Send the open toe dubonnet shoes from Aunt Mabel. I can use them as evening slippers. You see we usually have a formal party before graduation. As long as you are sending the suitcase you might as well include the gown and the shoes. If you can dig up a pair of earrings in my jewelry box that will go with the gown send them, too. Take your time. There is no rush on this matter.

The lights are being turned out and taps have blown so I must dash.
Love to all,
Bernice

* Avenger Field, Sweetwater, Texas, was the only all-female cadet air base in history. It was sometimes referred to as Cochran's Convent, and was of tremendous interest to many who really couldn't conceive of women conquering the new frontiers in the sky.

*Lake Sweetwater food preparation at our two and a half days off.*

*Velta Haney had a little red ford. We all piled into the car one way or another. Who ever heard of seat belts?*

*How about those legs? Some cheescake!*

# SEVEN

## ADVANCED TRAINING AND GRADUATION

July 2, 1944

Dear Mom,

Well, absolutely the most exciting thing has happened to me this weekend! Pyote Air Base, which is about 200 miles from here, invited some WASP down for a dance Saturday night and I was one of the fortunate twenty-seven to go. But let me tell you how. In a Flying Fortress B-17! Three pilots came here to call for us and fly us over and back. And they let us take turns flying the ship. I logged thirty-five minutes, which the captain signed for. It was absolutely perfect. The ship is very easy to fly, but the landings are something different and difficult and naturally we did not get

to do that. It takes a lot of strength to turn the wheel. After all you have four motors to control. It takes three men to land the ship.

We had a perfect time at the dance too. We stayed overnight and were treated royally. I am still glowing from the wonderful experience of flying as well as flying in a B-17. We did not get much sleep and I am just dead.

We started on navigation on Friday and Saturday. I was once again checked out in the AT-6, and was quite surprised to see that I could still fly the ship. After forty-five minutes dual he let me solo. We are starting to plot cross-country trips and are beginning to learn

*Merle P. Polhemus,*
*Navigation Instructor*

67

cross-country procedures. I am sure this phase will be lots of fun. I sure hope I won't get lost. My instructor is very nice. His name is Mr. Polhemus. I have seen pictures of the new B-29. We heard that two WASP have flown one. Can you imagine!

Taps are going to blow soon so I'll start signing off,

Much love to all,

Bernice

July 9, 1944

Dearest Mom,

I can see you are a very disillusioned person and need some facts very badly. I don't know where you got your information but it is all wrong. You see Jacqueline Cochran, General Arnold and Congressman Costello were the ones in back of the bill put before congress to make the WASP a part of the Air Force. As a matter of fact the bill is called the Costello Bill. Cochran has been very anxious indeed to have us made Army and so has General Arnold. She knew that Civil Service would not carry us on the budget much longer. Not only that, but a nice fat commission was in store for Cochran when we were made Army. It was all the fault of the rotten publicity the WASP have been getting and the fact that no one, or few came to our rescue and gave a true picture. Nothing else will be done now I am sure. The five classes that are left here will probably graduate and the WASP in the service will remain but no more new ones will be added. It's a very sad situation. *

I got your card from the Statue of Liberty and it sure seemed good to see the New York Skyline again. You know there is no city in Texas to even come near the size of any of our eastern cities–not even Dallas or Fort Worth.

I have a feeling this war will not be lasting long, I hope, and my position after the war is very insecure so I do want to save as much money as possible.

There are many extras we must buy to go with our uniforms and since Ruth wants to give me something and probably others will want to, in case they ask you, I am going to find out what extras we need and the prices and let them get me those things. Actually I shall have to buy them here because they must be regulation. One thing we buy here is a beautiful black over-the-shoulder pocketbook that I know you'll be crazy about. I also know you will love our uniforms. They are of exceptionally good quality.

I received my bag and thanks a million. We gobbled the cookies down in one night otherwise the ants get in them. The ants and bugs are awful. We have had a mouse living with us for the past three months. Her name is Jacqueline and she helps us consume any food we have in our bays.

No, Gen was not washed-out to teach others to be careful. They don't do things like that down here. I'll tell you the story as I got it from both sides when I see you.

So far navigation has been fun. It takes about six hours of preparation for a two and a half hour trip. We look like quite something going out to the ship with a computer, plotter, maps, radio charts, pencils, cushions, parachute, ruler, etc. You can hardly walk. You must be able to compute while en route–your gas consumption, actual speed, time of arrival, changes of route, procedures in case you are lost, wind corrections in the air and hundreds of other things–all very fascinating and interesting. Hope I don't get lost. I have a couple of dual cross-countries to go yet before they send me solo.

That's all for now.

Much love to all,<br>Bernice

*After D-day, June 6, 1944, the army began priming for the invasion of Europe. The flying programs of the Civil Aeronautics Administration War Training Service were being phased out to free those pilots for ground duty. They would then be subject to the draft. When these men heard of the legislation to militarize the WASP they deluged Congress with letters of protest. They were not concerned with the fate of the women, they were worried about the fate of the male pilots, who once released from the Civil Aeronautics Program, would be eligible for the draft.

NOTE: September 30, 1943, Representative John Costello of California introduced the WASP Militarization Bill, House Resolution 3358, which was a bill to provide for the appointment of female pilots in the Air Force of the Army. Following congressional protocol, the bill was referred to the Committee on Military Affairs for approval or recommendations. It was six months before this Committee held hearings. A longer bill House Resolution 4219 was heard June 20 and 21, 1944.

The debate did not focus on the WASP, but instead became a forum for Congress to placate the demands of the male civilian pilots' lobby, in which issues affecting not the WASP but the male pilots were raised and debated. Throughout the debate, it became clear that many members voting on the bill did not even understand that it was specifically about WASP militarization.

*June 20, 21, 1944, House of Representatives Hearings 1st row Jacqueline Cochran,*
*General "Hap" Arnold, Barbara Erickson (London).*
*2nd row: Nancy Love (behind General Arnold)*

It seemed that for many, their sole exposure to information about the WASP program was through the strongly biased and inaccurate report written by the Ramspeck Committee, or through opinion pieces and editorials published in newspapers or submitted to the Congressional Record. The Ramspeck Report took figures about WASP pilot training out of context, without comparing them to figures for male trainees and then developed negative conclusions about the statistics. It claimed the program would accelerate the accident and fatality rate even though the Army Air Force reports concluded the WASP had lower accident and fatality rates in training and on operational missions than did male pilots. His report went on with multitudes of incorrect information. There were even innuendos that Jacqueline Cochran had seduced General Arnold looking for a high commission.

Representative Costello argued "The sole purpose of this bill is simply this, to take these women who are now with the Army Air Force in a civilian capacity and convert them into a military capacity. That is the sole purpose of the WASP bill and nothing else. This should be done because these women at present are denied hospitalization; they are denied insurance benefits, and things of that kind to which, as military personnel, they should be entitled, and because of the work they are doing, they should be receiving at this time. May I point out that right now the Government can go out and spend $12,000 for training one of these women and, if you do not pass the bill, she can quit after she receives that training. You have spent $12,000 and you do not have anything to show for it. Might I emphasize that the cost of training one of these women is no different from the cost of training a man. It is approximately $12,000 for each. The cost for the uniforms is the same. The casualty rate is approximately the same. There has been no difference whatsoever between the men and the women."

The atmosphere of the congressional hearing was rather circus-like, with members of the male civilian pilots' lobby cheering, booing and making other outbursts. About 20 soldiers were asked to leave the gallery when they continued to applaud anti-WASP remarks from the floor.

**Finally the Bill was voted on:**
**188 yeas and 169 nays**
**73 representatives abstained**
**Defeated by 19 votes**

The House had effectively killed H.R. 4219. Not since the beginning of the war in 1941 had any legislation supported by the Army Air Force been turned down.

Army Air Forces Historical Studies No. 55–Women Pilots with the AAF 1941-44 indicates the fate of the militarization measure. From the record of the Congressional proceedings, "it appears that the supporters of the measure were too poorly organized and worked too slowly to match the legislative tactics of the opposition." The Army Air Force study is no whitewash, noting that women "were frequently confronted by hostility on the part of male pilots and commanding officers 'but' their very successful record of accomplishment has proved that in any future effort the nation can count on thousands of its young women to fly any of its aircraft. There is no doubt the failure to militarize women pilots was unfair to many WASP who had given good service. They were left without the benefits to which veteran's status would have entitled them, and the families of the girls who had been killed in the performance of their duties were denied the gratuities which they would have received as beneficiaries of military personnel."

**THIRTY-EIGHT WASP DIED**
**IN THE LINE OF DUTY**

Dear Mom,

I must use part of the ten days to get where I will be stationed which will probably be in the Middle West or the West.*  It will seem funny to be traveling around on a leave when traveling is probably what I will be doing so much of after graduation. By the way, we never know where we are going to be stationed but can request–not that you ever get what you ask for. At any rate, after much thought I believe I shall request to be stationed either on the West Coast or in the Midwest rather than the East. The way I feel is that after the war I may never have the opportunity to see the West, and now while I can, I shall.

Please let me know what you want to do because I have to make my arrangements early if I am going to try to arrange for a ride anywhere with the Air Transport Command (by bomber) and I also have to try to get a parachute. Gotta go eat now so, so long.

Much Love,<br>Bernice

* We were trying to make plans for Mom and Jackie to come to graduation, and for me to go home on the ten-day leave due us after graduation.

July 21, 1944

Dear Mom,

This is a very lovely day–it is pouring outside and therefore no flying. This comes as a welcome rest for a few hours. I am especially glad because, the night before last, I was awake the whole night vomiting. I think it was just a combination of heat and exhaustion. The next day I did not fly and today I feel as fine as ever.

So far I have been on two short,   two and a half hour solo cross-country trips, the others were dual. They are quite nice and fun but lots of work.

On my first solo cross-country I had an emergency landing at the airport where I was supposed to land. It was quite exciting. As I was letting down from 6,000 feet my motor would stop, then catch, then stop, then catch and pretty soon there was quite a bit of smoke, but no flames in the cockpit. I called the airport and told them I was coming in for an emergency landing so they could clear all traffic. I landed OK and when they examined the plane they found the right magnetos had cut out completely. It took a couple of hours to fix and then I returned to Sweetwater none the worse for wear. It was really fun. Nothing serious either. *

Much love to all,
Bernice

p.s. It seems incredible that on a routine two or two and a half hour flight in the AT-6 we cover from 200 to 300 miles. At times we figure our ground speed to be as high as 170 miles per hour or even more if we have a strong wind from the rear.

p.p.s. As far as my asking to be stationed either in the East or the West it really makes little or no difference because we go where they send us anyway. If I were stationed in the West I could get more flying time because the weather is better and after all flying is the reason I joined. Time alone will tell.

*In cases of forced landings, an accident or some emergency there was always an inquiry and the fear of being washed-out if found to be your fault. This is what was running through my mind when I had the emergency on my first solo AT-6 flight July 19 from Sweetwater to Wichita Falls to Harpersville and back to Sweetwater. Unless a fire had broken out in the plane I would not have considered bailing out even though I had a parachute.

July 25 , 1944

Dearest Mom,

The weather has been simply unbearably hot*.It is just suffocating. When not in class we just sit in the bays without a stitch of clothing on and the perspiration literally just drips from our bodies. Hope it gets cooler before you get here. We have been getting many military subjects along with our regular ground school. The latest attraction is a taste of chemical warfare. They tell us about different gases, their smells, effects, treatments, etc. Today we had gas mask drill, practicing putting them on and then they let us run through just a small bit of tear gas with and without the masks. We are also taking a course in first aid. They are taking up every bit of our free time.

Yesterday I went on a 450-mile cross-country. It took me four hours. We went to San Antonio, landed, refueled and came back here. I don't know yet where I go today.

By the way, I am again on a committee, this time to plan a party for W-6. You see it is the custom of the next class to graduate to give the graduation class a party the night before graduation. As a theme we are using Gay Nineties. Being on the committee, I will be going as a hostess. We are all making costumes to resemble those worn by the cancan girls. I think it will be kind of cute, don't you? .

We are really going to be busy now with cross-country and all. We will also be away from the field quite a bit, if I don't write too often don't worry.

Much love to all and thanks again, Hon.
Bernice

*We did not have television, the computers of today or air-conditioning nor was air-conditioning in general use in stores, movie houses, homes, etc.

NOTE: Altogether we had about ten cross-country flights, both day and night, in the AT-6. We also had cross-country in the Stearman which had no radio so we flew what is termed 'pilotage'. You were dependent upon your charts and calculations made prior to takeoff. On any cross-country, the first thing done was to draw lines on the chart denoting your route, making slash marks every ten miles. These were put there to remind you to check whether you were exactly on course. You would then use your E6B computer to calculate your compass heading. The slide rule face of the computer

is used to calculate time, speed, distance, fuel consumption and many other things. On the wind face side the course to be taken is drawn after learning the wind. Just before takeoff a visit to the weather office is mandatory to obtain wind direction, velocity, cloud coverage, visibility, etc. At this point the most favorable altitude is chosen. Walking to the airplane you are a

*Weather briefer giving conditions for a cross-country to Bev Frisbie, my instrument training flying buddy.*

sight to behold. You have a parachute, charts, flight plan, computer, pencils and personal items.

July 31, 1944

Dear Mom,

We came down here yesterday and leave tomorrow. You see we have to undergo pressure chamber tests for our reactions to high altitude flying. Will let you know how it turns out. We have some free time to wander around the city, which is quite a fascinating one. By the way, plan for my graduation date of September 7th.

Love,
Bernice

August 1, 1944

Hi Folks,

Just got back from San Antonio, 238 miles from here. We flew down in AT-6s on Sunday and came back today. The reason for the long stay is that we had to undergo pressure chamber tests and are not allowed to fly for twenty-four hours after you take the tests. We had some time to spend on our own and it was really swell.

San Antonio is a wonderful and very interesting city. I didn't get a chance to see very much. The historic Alamo Fort is in the center of town–"Remember the Alamo!" We saw that! The San Antonio River runs thru the center of town and has been canalled. It is really queer to see this strip of water and lovely grass and trees running through the main streets and around tall buildings. You can canoe around town. There are also the famous Breckenridge Park and the Japanese Gardens but I did not see these. San Antonio is listed as one of the most interesting cities in the United States.

It felt so good to be in a large city again with department stores and lights and cocktail lounges, etc. The streets are as crowded as those in New York but actually the size of the city is much smaller than Newark. However, it is tremendous for Texas.

About the pressure chamber tests–you see before we graduate, we must all go into a chamber where they 'take us up to 28,000 feet.' They do not actually fly us up, of course, but regulate the air so that it is the same density as that at various altitudes. Another girl and I volunteered to go up without our masks on so that they could show the rest of the girls what reactions take place when there is a lack of oxygen in the system. This lack of oxygen is called anoxia. It was really fun. You do not gasp for breath as one might imagine. As a matter of fact, you breathe quite easily and freely. However, you do feel dizzy as you go without oxygen and see bright spots before your eyes. They ask you to answer questions and your mind does not function rapidly–sometimes not at all. There is a long blank spot in my memory where they asked me several questions and I have absolutely no recollection of the incidents at all. It was as if I had been asleep and yet my eyes were open. However, they did not register what they saw.

Many of the things they told me to do in this condition I did, some incorrectly and some I would not do at all. It just proves to me quite a bit about the natural instincts. For instance, when they told me to put on my gas mask and by this time I was pretty near the blacking out stage I reached for it automatically. Of course, I was putting it on at a queer angle much to everyone's amusement and finally they had to help me. The second I breathed oxygen I snapped back to normal. I could hardly believe all the things went on that they claimed because it seemed as if no time had elapsed since my last coherent recollections. Some of the things were funny and I'll tell you about them when I see you. It was very interesting and I have found that anoxia would be a very pleasant way to die.

Much love to all,
Bernice


NOTE: When we completed the pressure chamber tests we were taken to our hotel, the White Plaza in the center of San Antonio via a military bus used by all from the base. During this trip we met some nice young Air Force officers who invited us out that evening. They picked us up at the hotel and took us to a unique nightclub called Seven Oaks in Alamo Heights that featured seating on platforms built into the trees (really beautiful) with a dance floor at ground level. Since San Antonio was a dry city you could not buy alcoholic beverages at a nightclub but were allowed to bring your own. The gentlemen brought a case of champagne and paid for set-ups.

*Irene B. Norris, Lt. A. S. Webb, Marion Hagen, Ruth Kent, Tom Hornbeck, Dale Jones, Betty Pettitt, Air Force1st Lt. "Doc" H. Enos, Bee Falk*

NOTE: Lieutenant "Doc" Lenos wrote on the picture folder, "To a very wonderful girl I met, with a line that has never been used before with champagne and music. I think more will come of this."–We never met again but a good time was had by all.

August 7, 1944

Dear Mom,

This is simply wonderful. We have finished ground school.

Until they give us some more military subjects, and our written instrument test, we have some time to ourselves.

You see, long cross-countries have started and groups of twelve go off in three directions. With them go an Army officer, the establishment officer and two instructors. My instructor is due to go on the western trip (to California) tomorrow. That means that for three days I will have no flying.

Of course there is plenty to do around here. I have to get all my books in order and do some studying, etc. I am not scheduled for any long cross-countries this week but expect to go on one next week. Don't know for sure yet. I believe we'll start night flying soon.

Can't wait to see you guys. Bring plenty of cool clothes. It is hotter than the devil down here.

We are beginning to get things for our uniform. Some of the things we must have and have to buy for ourselves are;

| | |
|---|---|
| white shirts | shoes |
| blue shirts | gloves |
| socks | neckties |

Things we do not have to have, but may get if we want;

pocketbook (which is beautiful and you'll love it)

belt

insignia and other incidentals

Of course we have to buy these things here because they are all regulation.

By the way, one day in Sweetwater is loads of time for me to be able to show you all there is to see in the town and at Avenger so spend as much time as you can sightseeing in California, OK?

Our party was a great success. The cancan girls were very cute and the costumes were nice.

Enclosed is a bond.


August 14, 1944

Dear Mom,

Yes, the stationery is correct.* You see I started my 2,000-mile cross-country today and this is where we are spending the night. It is about 300 miles from Atlanta and I believe that will be our next stop.

We flew five and a half hours today and about 800 miles. I am tired so will leave out details. We are all practically deaf from flying with the radio and following beams where we can. First we went to Greenville, Texas–east of Dallas, then to Stuttgart, Arkansas–east of Little Rock and then to Meridian, Georgia–west of Atlanta. This country is certainly different from Texas. There are lovely large trees. Also much rice is grown hereabouts. We can see the irrigation ditches clearly from the air.

Now before I fall asleep sitting up, the main reason for my writing is to tell you to turn in your bus tickets and let me make train reservations for you. I want to put what I save on carfare home towards your train tickets (Pullman if I can get it). Either that or you must promise that you will travel by bus, only during the day, and sleep in a hotel at night. By this time you have had a taste of bus travel and will not want another so please wire your

OK to make Pullman reservations for you and Jackie.

Much love and goodnight,

Bernice

\* Lamar Hotel, Meridian, Mississippi.

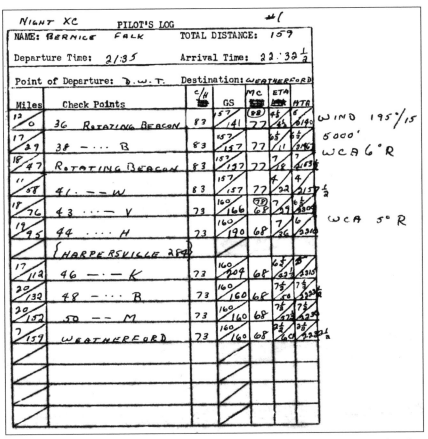

*Before any cross-country we had to prepare a log giving all navigation details. The one above is for an AT-6 flight which had radio. When going on a cross-country in a Stearman which had no radio and was open cockpit, there was much to be concerned about. A careless move and the chart and all your notes could blow out of the aircraft.*

NOTE: September 1, 1944, was my first night solo cross-country from Sweetwater to Weatherford and return. The Morse code we noted on our logs is for light beacons, which we call 'light lines.' Every ten miles a beacon flashes a one-letter code, which can be found on our charts enabling pilots to know where they are. After one hundred miles the code sequence starts again. The sentence we used to remember the order of the code letters was "<u>W</u>hen <u>U</u>ndertaking <u>V</u>ery <u>H</u>ard <u>R</u>outes <u>K</u>eep <u>D</u>irections <u>B</u>y <u>G</u>ood <u>M</u>ethods."

Dearest Mom,

I am going to try and make tentative reservations for you at the Blue Bonnet Hotel for the 3rd 4th and 5th. Go to the Blue Bonnet when you get into town. If you tell me what bus you are coming in on I shall try to meet it. Maybe a last minute telegram will do. I'll do my best to get off post to meet you. If you don't see me it might be a good idea to telephone me from the bus station–try 2036, 2037 or 2038. It may take some time to locate me so don't get impatient. If I am flying on the flight line they may not be able to reach me. Tell the person who answers that you are my mother and it is important that they look real good for me or call me off the flight line if that is where I am.

Some of the kids have been to Juarez so let me warn you. It is a Mexican border town and they try to take advantage of tourists. Be especially careful of perfumes because they really gyp you on that. I might suggest not even buying any perfume. One other thing I would like, if you happen to see them, is a pair of huaraches. They are sort of a woven leather with leather soles–perfectly flat. I believe they cost about $2 or $3.

If you do go to San Antonio you might stay at the White Plaza Hotel. It is a small hotel in the center of town. We had lovely rooms when we stayed there and it amounted to about $2.25 per person per night. The Gunter Hotel is directly across the street from the White Plaza and may not be as expensive but is not quite as nice–at least the rooms we saw in the non-air-conditioned part were not as nice. The Gunter Coffee Shop is a pretty good place to eat.

Oh yes, one more thing. We started night flying and I soloed much to my surprise! We do landings with and without lights. It really is quite an experience flying at night. I have to go on two, two-hour cross-country night trips Monday and Tuesday night.

Can't wait to see you both and show you the field and all.

Much love and kisses, and have a good time.

Please be careful.

Bernice

NOTE: It had become tradition for the class before the one graduating to give a party the night before graduation, usually at the Blue Bonnet Hotel in the Avengerette Club. Class 44-8 gave us one which they called "NAUGHTY-CAL DANCE for those Rip Roarin' Pirates 44-W-7"

Each graduating class sang a song. Ours was to the tune of:
WE AIN'T GONNA BE HERE MUCH LONGER
> Who's that yonder flying like an Ace?
> She rides the skies with a lazy grace
> Dressed in blue and as proud as can be
> No, you don't have to guess; it's 44-7 you see
> Oh, do you have wings? Oh yes, my pet!
> It's a long, long way and we earned 'em you bet!

## THE CLASS OF 44-7 BEFORE GRADUATION

August 2, 1944 Sweetwater, Texas. WASP (Women Airforce Service Pilots), Class of 44-7.

| | | | |
|---|---|---|---|
| 1. Ruth Reilly | 16. Bernice Falk | 31. Adelaide Shafer | 46. Margaret Shafer |
| 2. Sylvia Miller | 17. Bernice Dannefer | 32. Margaret Parish | 47. Eileen Wright |
| 3. Mimi Caffery | 18. Patricia Blackburn | 33. Anne Cawley | 48. Ola Rexroat |
| 4. Anne Pedroncelli | 19. Dorothy A. Smith | 34. Opal Hicks | 49. Mary Storm |
| 5. Muriel Rath | 20. Ellen Wimberly | 35. Mary Putman | 50. Betty Jo Streff |
| 6. Vivyan Williams | 21. Betty Eagan | 36. Frances Winters | 51. Edith Smith |
| 7. Mary Jean Barnes | 22. Eleanor Gunderson | 37. Winnie Jones | 52. Hulda Chilcoat |
| 8. Betty Roth | 23. Margarete McGrath | 38. Penny Halladay | 53. Dorothy Sorenson |
| 9. Carol Nicholson | 24. Margaret Weiss | 39. Jean Landa | 54. Mary Quist |
| 10. Irene Norris | 25. Marjorie Neyman | 40. Virginia Mullen | 55. Joan Smythe |
| 11. Nancy Nordhoff | 26. Nona Holt | 41. Laura Jane Harris | 56. Edith Upson |
| 12. Iola Clay | 27. Betty Jane Overman | 42. Virginia Krum | 57. Mary Ellen Walker |
| 13. Geraldine Bowen | 28. Alberta Paskvan | 43. Nancy Conklin | 58. Annie Jean Henry |
| 14. Berverly Frisbie | 29. Grace Ashwell | 44. Virginia Bradley | 59. Velta Haney |
| 15. Mildred Eckert | 30. Betty Pettitt | 45. Lila Moore | |

*September 8, 1944, Graduation of 44-7. 98 entered training, 59 graduated. Dorothy Sorenson, Jacqueline Cochran, Mary Helen Crowe, Mrs. Leota Deaton, Lt. Col. Roy P. Ward, Commanding Officer 2563rd AAF Base Unit, Avenger Field, Sweetwater, Texas. Principal speaker Lt. Col. Roy P. Ward. Band: Big Springs Bombardier School.*

*Along with those coveted wings, we received the official diploma.*

*Jackie, Bee and Mom at graduation, September 8, 1944*

# From Lloyd in France

September 17, 1944

Dear Bernice,

How happy I felt when I received your last letter with the announcement of your graduation. Honestly, Bernice, I really am very proud of you. The show was completely yours and you did marvelously. One of the things I want to do when I get home is do some flying with you. I'll sign the weather clearance.

Naturally, you will want to know how do I like France?
As compared to England–well, you can't compare because I can't speak French, which makes it difficult to talk to people. Life here as compared to what I had in England is, of course, much less one of ease. There we had such things as electricity any time of day. Here, one hour at night—maybe more, maybe less. There we had heat–depending on where you lived. Here, coal is a scarcity. Now, I am living in an officer's billet, which consists of a fairly good-sized house, no hot water–we have a gas heater but haven't discovered the combination to turn on the gas. It is available I believe–but how to get it is another question. Haven't shaved in hot water since I left England.

This is the second place that I have lived in since coming over. The other place had its advantages. More electricity–more food (excellently cooked by French chefs)–more beverages for which France is famous. Food is scarcer here, and though the people don't look starved they don't look well-fed. What it is like in a big city like Paris, I have yet to discover.

France, as a whole, is pretty much messed up by the war. Transportation is bad since we seem to have done a very good job of messing it up before and after the invasion. Jerry did some damage also in his retreat. I have been through some towns where the war raged bitterly during the first month or two before the big break-through. They are practically nonexistent. And when I say that, well, I really mean it–masses of just plain rubble. Otherwise, areas where the Germans did not make a stand, but just beat the hell away are practically untouched. This place is a very good example. What could have been done had we not moved as rapidly as we did! That would be very easy to imagine once having seen some of these places. No kidding, it would be better to build new towns than salvage the old. But on the whole, all such places are comparatively few.

The war news certainly has been wonderful–better perhaps than most expected–certainly better than I ever dreamt two months ago. Strange how suddenly things happen.

You asked about robot bombs. It was not considered the thing to do to write home about them while back there. But I saw and heard too many.

Again, again and again–Congratulations, Sis! I'm really proud of you!
Loads of love and scads of luck,
Lloyd

Often I am asked why the WASP at that time were not doing anything to help us be inducted into the Army Air Corps. Remember we were scattered throughout the U.S. or were still in training. Also we had been advised to do nothing. I think the reason for that is because General Arnold had never been denied any of his requests when he went before Congress.

# EIGHT

## ACTIVE DUTY

September 24, 1944

Dear Folks,

Well here I am at my first assignment, Pecos Air Force Base, Pecos, Texas. Believe me I was pleasantly surprised that everyone is so nice. Indeed I am fortunate to find myself at such a nice post. There are other girls here from other classes and two others from W-7, Irene Norris and Joan Smythe, both from Flight 2. They are very nice girls and lots of fun.

All the WASP stay at the Civilian Housing Projects on post. These are one-story red brick buildings with one, two and three person apartments. The three of us from W-7 have an apartment together that is very nice. There is not much furniture because it hasn't arrived yet. There are three separate bedrooms, each containing a bed, a chest of drawers and a closet. The living room has no furniture. The kitchen has a small four-burner stove, a new all white refrigerator, lovely sinks, lots of shelf space and a very large pantry and storage space. It really is a very lovely place.

We are going to do some cooking providing we have enough time. Today we had a grand house cleaning session and made our own supper. Tomorrow we'll make breakfast and perhaps supper. We have to provide our own dishes and cooking utensils but some of the previous tenants have left us a few things.

I had to get my uniform pressed and then report. This took quite some time because there are many forms to fill out, people to meet and many other things to attend to.*

As for the flying–it seems when the girls arrived last month, they were put through an instructor's course that was really swell. They got night flying, formation flying and night formation flying as well as other routine flying and ground school. That course has been discontinued because they need the instructors for the cadets. Things are pretty crowded around here–

some instructors have as many as nine students.

The job the WASP are doing here is test hopping. When an airplane has been repaired, it must be tested. The airplanes are called UC-78s or AT-17s (the same plane). I shall send you a picture of one. They only have 225-horsepower in each engine and are primarily used as trainers for the larger bi-motor and four-motored airplanes. Saturday, I went up  as copilot with another WASP.  You have to fly fifty hours as copilot before you can be checked out as first pilot. Since we can't take the instructors course as the others did, we shall have to try to get as much as we can from the other WASP.

Major Rizzo, our immediate superior, is a swell guy. He is going to do all he can to get us qualified dual instruction of some sort. He said he would rather have ten WASP than a bunch of lieutenants because the WASP are conscientious, work hard and try to do all they can instead of doing as little as possible.

So far, so good and I hope it keeps up. I'll sign off for now, with much         love and please take care of yourself.

Much love,

Bernice

*When entering a base for the first time, it was customary  to appear before the C.O. (Comanding Officer) and introduce yourself. We had formal calling cards, wore our dress uniforms including white gloves and, of course, did all the required  saluting.

*Emblem of Pecos Army Air Force Base*

*UC78 Manufactured by Cessna.*

NOTE: Pecos Army Air Field was a twin-engine advanced flight school. We flew the Cessna Bobcat manufactured by Cessna Aircraft as a transitional twin-engine aircraft designated AT-I7 (Advanced Trainer) and UC-78 (Utility Cargo). It had two 225-horsepower Jacob engines. It also had many nicknames–Bamboo Bomber, Useless 78, Double-breasted Cub, Shakey Jakey. The jobs assigned to the WASP were as engineering test and utility pilots. After we were disbanded December 20, 1944, Pecos became a B-25 bomber base January 1, 1945. Had we remained, I would have been flying B-25s.

<u>Lloyd's Letter from Outside of Paris to His Fiancée, Elea</u>

September 30, 1944

Hello Sweetheart,

Don't be amazed at the size of this large paper. It is some German stationery, which among other things, they left behind in their rather hasty retreat. It really is not bad paper, though what they would do with this stuff is beyond me.

Paris, Darling, is really a beautiful city and I would love to be able to take you there–probably a long time from now into the future. I wish that you could have been with me to enjoy it, it beats London–there is just no comparison. Paris is off-limits to American soldiers except those who are actually stationed in the city, (naturally) and those who go in on business. Why of course "we had business"–namely sightseeing. We made out all right though.

When we arrived at the edge of the city we were picked up by a civilian who drove us to the nearest Métro station. This is the Parisian underground or subway system. We were more or less surprised to find that it was in operation. And also surprised that no one asked for a ticket–even when we left at the destination. Later we found that the entire underground system is absolutely free to men in uniform. An amazing city! Incidentally, the Métro system reminds me more of New York's than that of London. Métro is not as deep as in London, nor do they need escalators. The Parisian subway is supposed to be the greatest in the world, but probably due to the war and shortage of power they do not go at very great speeds.

We got off at L'Etoile, which we learned later, means 'The Star'– named because of the large number of roads that lead from this large circular intersection. In the center is located the large Arc de Triomphe–built to commemorate Napoleon's victories. Directly under the center of the Arc is located the Tomb of the Unknown Soldier decorated with flowers. Fresh ones are placed there every day by various military organizations. On the walls facing the interior of the Arc are lists of names of Napoleon's victories and his most able generals and men. Around the Arc is a large broad traffic circle. The famous boulevard–the Champs-Elysées begins here.

We wanted to see the Eiffel Tower–so took a turn into the Avenue Kleber, which brought us to the square called the Trocadéro. Here presented a magnificent view of the tower from a group of buildings called the Palais de Chaillot–more properly known as the Trocadéro –since the old building the Palais replaced went by that name. This Palais overlooked a broad wide park with beautiful fountains (not operating) and provisions for night lighting, probably in various colors. The next thing in the view from the Palais is the Pont d'Iena–one of several beautiful bridges that cross the Seine. This was named after one of the victories of Napoleon. Then came the Eiffel Tower itself, which is about 900 feet high–and we later learned contains as many steps to the top. There is an elevator but it was not operating at the time–and we were lazy.

On we walked, until we crossed the Seine once again to find the Place de la Concorde–a large traffic square–an Egyptian obelisk in the center. The Champs-Elysées ends here (or begins depending on which way you
come). There is also the entrance to the Jardin Des Tuilleries–a royal garden that was closed at present to the public. Here in the center of the Concorde

we were vigorously welcomed to Paris by Jacqueline–our ten year old kissing mademoiselle, she tagged along for awhile–showing us an old German tank that was put out of action by the 77th Infantry in the last days of the German occupation of Paris. We gave her some chewing gum and candy we had with us–finally, she took her leave–turning every few steps to wave goodbye until she disappeared around a corner.

We continued on our way passing the Madeleine Church–originally built by Napoleon (one would almost think that the whole of Paris is a monument for Napoleon) and into our first and last inquisitive MP.* Our story held water and on we went–asking at various photo shops for film and pestering perfumeries for Chanel #5. Film yes (I now have a considerable stock) Chanel–impossible. I have some perfume but I am debating whether to send it through the mail.

We visited the Louvre Palace–now partially used as an art museum– until the war forced them to take away most of the treasures. The Vénice de Milo was there but now the Germans have it. Next we found the Opéra–a large impressive building–the interior of which I would like to see when and if the opera productions are ever begun again during the war.

We asked our way to Notre Dame Cathedral. It is located on a large island in the Seine known as the Cité (from which our word city probably derives). This is the oldest part of Paris–even existed before the Romans made their appearance under Julius Caesar. The interior of the cathedral is fairly dark (the main stained glass windows have been removed because of the war) and curtains hung in their place. The cathedral itself is quite old and since it was built just at the beginning of the Renaissance period does not look as beautiful as the later Gothic style churches.

We ate lunch while sitting on the banks of the Seine's concrete and stone embankments. Lunch consisted of one box of R-rations that we had brought with us. We cannot get food in Paris unless actually stationed here. For our thirst we used beer that was obtainable at many cafes located all over the place. Some was good–some bad.

After awhile at Notre Dame we went looking for the famed Bastille that the French are always storming whenever anything big happens. Well, Darling, to say the least we were somewhat disappointed. We expected to find an old well-weathered fortress, complete with dungeons, moats and drawbridges. Instead we found a tall monument in the center of a large traffic circle erected on the former sight of the original Bastille. Later we found that when the French people stormed it during the Revolution in 1789 they meant it. It was torn down then. Why doesn't anyone tell me these things!

The people of this city are very friendly. The ones with whom we had dinner are a typical example. Whenever we stopped to ask someone how to get to a certain place, we were always sure to gather a little knot of three or four others who would try to help us. If someone were passing us who could speak English, he would stop and tell us what we wanted to know. Once we asked for a post office since Capt. Bundgaard wanted to buy some stamps for his father-in-law's collection. We were trying to get across what we wanted to a man on a street corner when an elderly lady stopped and not only told us where it was in English but also led us to it and even negotiated his purchases. Yes, the people are quite friendly. This lady told us that "Paris is dead now." What must it be like when it is alive?

I believe I have written about the Sacré-Coeur–a fairly modern church built way up on a hill. It is fairly new and looks it.

Another thing we did in one of our times in Paris was to go to a French motion picture–it was on the liberation of France. Though the monologue was in French, the pictures were interesting–especially those taken by an FFI** cameraman before American troops entered–showing street fights–erection of barricades in the streets by digging up the cobblestones and piling up everything from old automobiles to iron beds– also German tanks maneuvering in the streets and other such bits of the Parisian liberation. I hope it will be shown in America because it is really worthwhile. Though the speaking we could not understand, the reactions of the audience were very interesting. A great deal of applause at the drop of a hat–Churchill, Roosevelt, Stalin, de Gaulle–practically everyone of any note and others whom we did not recognize but no doubt were well known to the French. There are not many motion picture houses in operation in Paris. Consequently, there are long queues before those that are open. For soldiers, the doorman will lead you to the head of the line, will buy your tickets (with your money, of course) and you go right in. Voila! Paris!

Spent an evening with Capt. Bundgaard trying out a few of their cabarets and cafes. Prices were high in some and low in others. Imagine paying $.90 for a glass of beer in one place and $.10 a few doors away. Reason–the first calls itself a cabaret–that gives it the right to charge more. I guess New York City is the same way. This all was after the vain attempt on our part to obtain tickets for the Fred Astaire show that was playing there at the time for Army personnel.

This briefly is the highlight of our visits.

> For now,
>> Love,
> Lloyd

* American Military Police.
** Forces Francaises de L'Interieur–the French resistance network organized to overthrow the German forces occupying France during World War II.

October 1, 1944

Dear Mom and Dad,

We have really been very busy this week and it seems we have been here longer. Our day is filled up. We go to instructor's school at 7:45 a.m. and fly all morning. Then in the afternoon we fly, as with the other girls, they are sending us to instructor's school to learn how to fly the UC-78 or AT-17 (same airplane). It being a twin-engine plane, there are many things to learn. I believe we will get about forty hours in school plus some ground school. I like it very much. I have a swell instructor who is very patient, conscientious and thorough.

As far as social life is concerned, there is too much of it. You can have ten dates a night if you desire. They are nice boys–most of them–and we can have lots of fun, but being a WASP we must act like ladies and watch our step because of gossip. There was a formal dance at the Officer's Club last night and I went. Had a good time. There is a swimming pool on the post and yesterday afternoon I spent swimming and getting burned. The post has everything you need–practically. The town of Pecos is very small. We are allowed to wear civilian clothes in the evening and when not on duty.

Our domestic life is fairly good. We do not have much time to shop, the grocery store is far away and it usually closes before we get home. We do manage to get our own breakfast and once in a while our dinner. Time element is the big problem.

Oh yes, we have a theater on the post. Only fifteen cents admission. Saw a good show the other night, Arsenic and Old Lace, taken from the stage show. It's a riot! See it if it comes around your way.

Take care of yourselves and much love,

Bernice

October 5, 1944

Dear Mom,

Perhaps by this time you have read in the papers about the WASP being disbanded December 20, 1944. Naturally, we have all expected it sooner or later but needless to say it came as a blow. Now the big question is what to do? First, I am going to try to get a job flying somewhere. We are all going to write to aircraft companies and try to get jobs as test pilots or copilots on some of the larger crafts. Just how this will turn out we don't know but it's worth a try. For the next couple of months I shall be rather busy writing letters and chasing around the country trying to make contacts so if you do not hear from me too regularly you will know why.

We are going to school as usual and copiloting, too. All of us are going to fly just as much as we can so we can build up our flying time. Also trying to get my commercial. We don't know as yet whether we will get any benefits. Nor do we know about keeping our uniforms. Time will tell.

My love to all,
Bernice

October 16, 1944

Dear Mom,

I spent a wonderful Saturday night in Dallas. You see, we are allowed to go on weekend cross-countries every so often. As yet I have not finished the instructors course and so cannot apply for my own ship but two of the pilots were going to Fort Worth and took me as passenger. From there I took a bus to Dallas arriving in Dallas at 6:30, Saturday evening.

The main reason for my going there was to see a person by the name of Louis Ralnick. He is from Bayonne and is one of Irv's gang whom I knew well before the war. Irv wrote me he was here and since I had the chance to go to Dallas I took advantage of it. We had a simply marvelous time. Went out to dinner and then to some friend's house. You see Lou's work carries him all over the country and he leaves Dallas on Friday. He is a very nice chap and I had lots of fun and enjoyed his company immensely.

Your idea of California is good. I rather thought of exhausting all flying job possibilities in the West and Middle West before returning home even if it means missing Christmas. I cannot afford to cross the country too often even by bus. I have been making inquires all around but have gotten no concrete help. It seems the most sensible thing is to go directly to companies in person. Gerry Ashwell has access to a list of aircraft companies, and whom to see or write to. As soon as she gets this, she will send me a copy and I shall have something to work with. I have ten days leave coming  and may take a couple of days off in the future to job hunt, if I think it worthwhile. Meanwhile I fly as much as I can. Shall tell you more details in my next.

Meanwhile, take care and love to all,

B.

October 19, 1944

Dearest Mom,

The food sure looks good. As a matter of fact I had some of the cheese with tomatoes (my favorite–grilled) for lunch today. I am having a bit of domestic trouble at this point. I told you that three of us live together and that we were going to all chip in together and buy food etc. Well it seems that we were buying food and kids were coming in with their dates at night making eggs etc. and we never had any food. I would get something for supper and the other kids would invite fellows and couples for dinner, etc.

I decided, no more, and promptly proceeded to eat at the club. However, eating every meal out is quite expensive and the food is not good. The other kids don't pitch in to do the shopping or anything either so our little deal has sort of petered out.

However, this  a.m. I decided I wanted to eat at least a couple of meals at home so I told the kids that I thought it would be best if each of us did her own shopping, cooking, cleaning up etc. I don't think they are too happy about it but I don't want to do all the work for three people. It's easier for just me. I'll see now if I can keep some food in the house under these conditions. If not, I'll just eat out and forget all about it.

Love to all,

Bernice

October 26, 1944

Dear Mom,

Am enclosing a bond. This is being written in haste because there has been plenty to do the last few days. As you know I am trying hard to get as much flying time in as possible. The cooking of dinners has not worked out too well because I usually get down from flying about 7:30 and by the time I get into some clothes to go home, it's so late and I'm so tired that I can hardly move. Therefore, I usually dine at the club at night.

Today I received the moccasins. I can hardly tell you how much I really love them. I have a callus on the bottom of my right foot that bothers me and the moccasins sure feel good. Not only that but it is getting quite cold at night and in the mornings and we have only a cement floor at home so it really will feel good.

I have been thinking about what to do after December and have gotten several good ideas. I am convinced that they are good and you know that I am not one to exaggerate my ideas–being more on the conservative side. I asked Betty to keep her eyes open for a flying job of some sort and it seems that she knows of a couple of fellows who want to open a small airport in New Jersey. They want her to stay there (or something like that– get the details from her) and she can have all the flying time she wants and they will pay her carfare. Of course, I could never work for this, nor would I. But if these guys have the equipment and some money and would want to let me work up some sort of business, I am sure I could do plenty. You see, right now there would be a great demand for a 'Taxi of the Air Service' to take people on short notice to wherever they want to go. Then there is always the need for freight to be delivered in a hurry. Of course, for much of this large ships would be necessary. But you could start in a small way and then work up to larger ships. There are hundreds of miscellaneous jobs that could be done by plane and now is the time to start. I have written to Betty about my ideas (no doubt she will read you the letter) and asked her to approach these guys and feel them out, but not to divulge any of my ideas.

I still think I shall take a trip to California before leaving this part of the country and sort of look over the situation for flying jobs the country over.

Love and kisses

B.

November 4, 1944

Dear Mom,

No doubt you are wondering about the stationery and California, etc. Well, the most exciting thing ever has happened to me and I guess I am really a very, very lucky girl. You see a couple of ground school instructors from Pecos had to make an administrative trip visiting various fields from Pecos to the coast. They do not fly and a pilot was needed. For some unknown reason Major Rizzo gave me the job. It is one that many people wanted, and at long last I am seeing California–if only from the air.

We left Pecos yesterday morning at 5:00 a.m. and first went to Deming, New Mexico, then Marana, Arizona, (near Tucson), then Las Vegas, Nevada, and finally, Bakersfield, California, where we stayed over night.

I guess you know who are stationed at Bakersfield–Gerry Ashwell and Eleanor Gunderson (the tall blond who lived in my bay at Sweetwater). You can imagine all the shouts of joy and chattering that took place at this reunion. Gosh it was so good to see the kids again. I sure wish I were stationed here with them. All the kids are swell at their field and work together so nicely. Oh well, I do get more flying than they do and the people at Pecos are nice so I really have no complaint. Not only that but they are on the coast where bad weather is quite common and they are surrounded by mountains over which they are not allowed to fly. My flight here was very nice and I enjoyed flying over mountains (the first time I ever have). Right now we are in Marana, which is a twenty-five-minute flight from Bakersfield and it looks as if we will not be able to fly out of this valley today because of bad weather. That means I'll be able to spend more time with the kids, this does not displease me one bit.

Yesterday was really rather rugged. I flew nine hours. We would just have time to rush into these various places–while I made out clearances, they attended to their business, and then off we would go again. We passed through two time zones.

Gerry Ashwell plans to go home for Christmas, but Gunderson intends to stay on in California and start job-hunting–working her way east. In other words her intentions are the same as mine and so we plan to meet in Los Angeles after December 20. She, being so near to Los Angeles, is going to see what she can about jobs before the 20th and also something about a cheap place for us to stay while we are in Los Angeles. Do we know anyone around there very well? I think she has some distant relatives there but am not sure.

Love to everybody and take it easy,

Bernice

NOTE: During the trip flying the two ground school officers to other flight schools around the country so they could compare curriculums we had an interesting adventure.

On the trip from Marana, Arizona, back to Pecos we had planned to RON (remain over night). While having dinner in Marana we met some pilots from Pecos who said they were flying back that night and why didn't we join them. They suggested we would not have to bother with the navigation but just follow them We all agreed since we were anxious to return to home base. We lined up behind the other ships and all took off closely behind one another. The taillight of the aircraft is white. We were doing just fine following this bright white light in front of us when we suddenly realized it was not a taillight–but a star!!! There was much scrambling for charts.

With the help of the light lines* we were able to find our position and the way back to Pecos. We landed along with the other ships so no one was the wiser concerning what had actually happened. I learned a valuable lesson from this experience. Never allow others to do your navigating!!!

*Light lines were explained in Chapter 7

November 13, 1944

Dear Mom,

 I arrived home from California on Tuesday night. We were weathered in until Tuesday afternoon and as soon as we were cleared I flew back to Pecos (six hours and ten minutes) flying all afternoon and night to make it. The trip was nice and it was quite an experience flying over mountains. The trip from Taft, California, to Santa Anna (just below Los Angeles) took us over some of the most beautiful mountains I have ever seen. They had snow on top and there were many trees. We were over clouds a good deal of the time, which made it even more beautiful.

 Thanks for the information about the airport opening in Morristown. This would be a good location and not only that but the country around there is lovely. As soon as I get home I am going to look up all of these things—that is unless I get a job somewhere else first. As I have said before, my idea is to try and locate in California so you can move out here. That is why I am going to try the West Coast first.

 Now I am keeping house with five other WASP who are more conscientious about it. We have good meals, share the work and expenses, and have a good time, too. It is much better this way. We do all of our cooking in the apartment of one of the other girls.

 Thanks for the reassurance of always having a home and you. That I know but I want to be able to make a decent salary so I can see you very nicely retired in California. You know, if we ever did get to California Jackie could go to the University of Southern California tuition free.

Love to all,<br>Bernice

November 20, 1944

Dear Mom,

 Exactly one month from today is the big day. Boy, it really is beginning to hit. All of us are feeling kind of blue already. It is going to be one big heartache. There are lots of things that will have to be done. We just received word that they are going to allow us to keep one slack set (summer or winter), one dress uniform (summer or winter) and the overcoat. The rest we may buy (that we own) at 50% discount. I shall buy just a very few things such as a pair of gloves, and a couple of zoot suits (which will amount to about $5 apiece). I thought I would either sell one suit to Betty or give it to her for a birthday present if she would like it. I shall spend about $20 because I really can't afford much more than that. Not only that, I don't know what kind of a job I'll be getting and I may not need more work clothes of this type. I am going to keep the winter slack suit (it is of good woolen material) and shall keep the winter dress suit if they ever issue me mine in the right size (so far I have not received my winter dress suit). If there is anything of my equipment you would like or think I should buy let me know before the 20th. The winter slack suits cost something like $15 for the jacket and $9 for the slacks. The winter dress suit costs about $40.

I have written twenty-five letters to different aircraft companies all over the United States and so far have received nothing but noes. It looks kind of bleak but I still intend to embark on a venture in search of a flying job.

I believe we will be allowed to travel by military aircraft for one month after the 20th of December. I hope this is true and I shall try to profit by it if only just to jaunt around and see some of the country. Don't you agree? If I need money while on the job search, you can cash in some of my bonds and put the money in the bank. Don't worry. I'll let you know if I go broke. I am going to look on all of this as some escapade I might never have had had I not joined the WASP. If I have to come back to a secretarial job I guess it won't be too bad. I always do have that to fall back on. The reason my typing is so messy now is because I am rushing but I know I can still do a good job of it. As a matter of fact, I can always get a job here in Pecos as a secretary but I wouldn't take that kind of a job in Texas.

We had some bad weather for a few days and I spent that time writing to companies for a job but now I am trying to get in as much flying time as possible and also trying to enjoy all the wonderful social life there is to offer around the Officer's Club in the evenings. .

Love to all and take care of yourself,

B

November 23, 1944

Dear Mom:

First of all Happy Thanksgiving and very appropriately your package was received today. Golly the dress is just absolutely perfect. I can't tell you how much I like it. The color is simply beautiful and it is the type that I can wear at any time at all. Let me tell you something really funny. You see I had carried the package with me from the post office to the Officers' Club whence I was indulging in a glass of beer with someone who had taken me to Thanksgiving dinner. I was anxious to see what you had bought so at the bar I opened the package. Of course I turned all different colors upon seeing the pink panties staring this Officer and myself in the face. Believe me, I was a bit embarrassed but all I could say was "Oops" and I run into a secluded corner to finish opening the package. Of course, the Officer (one Lt. Gilbert, by the way, from Mass.) just laughed himself sick more at the "Oops" than the fact that I had received pink panties. Believe me, it was worth it because we all had a good laugh.

By the way, we worked today just the same. The weather was bad and I got stuck above some clouds not able to see the field a couple of times but all was well because I got down o.k. It was kind of exciting.

I have some good news. There is a B29 pilot from Pyote (which is 20 miles from here) who lives in Los Angeles and who comes over to Pecos quite often. He is sort of in with a gang with whom I used to go around before they were shipped out and yesterday he told me that he was looking for someone who wanted to go to L.A. around the 20th of December because he has to get his car home since he is being shipped out of Pyote. Naturally I grabbed at the opportunity because this solves my luggage problem for the time being. He says he has plenty of gas and will pay for the expenses to Cal. All I have to do is deliver the car to his home. Since he is a good friend, I am sure he will say it is o.k. for me to use the car while I am in California. Some one of these days I shall ask him. By the way, he has money. His folk have a horse farm and mansion in Tennessee and from the pictures of his folk I have seen, it looks as if they are somehow connected with the movies. I'll ask him.

One more favor, - Would you send any old alarm clock that you have kicking around the house to me since I shall probably need it in L.A. If there is none, don't bother.

Here I am at the end of the sheet so I'll sign off with lots of love and will write as soon as I again have a chance.

Love, Bernice


November 30, 1944

Dear Mom,

Now that I am going into civilian life again I'll need silk stockings. I left quite a few pairs at home when I left for Sweetwater both new and used and would appreciate it if you would send them to me. Do not buy me any new ones because if I don't have enough I can pick some up inexpensively in Juarez.

Nothing much new except that we are all flying as much as we can and are trying to prepare for our commercial licenses. I am also going to try and get my instructor's certificate and perhaps my instrument rating although this would take lots of studying and practice and I really don't have the time right now. I am still writing letters to various companies as I receive leads but have heard nothing favorable from any of them.

It is very late. I usually don't get to eat supper before about 8:00 or 8:30 at night.

Love to all,
B.

December 3, 1944

Dear Mom,

Gosh, I can't tell you how very, very sorry I am for all the times I complained about no college education. Since leaving home I realize how unimportant this is in view of the fact that I have an education now that all the money in the world could not buy. With my WASP diploma I can earn as much, if I find the right job, as a person with a college education. So please, Hon, do not fret any longer over the subject. You see I'm grown up now and far away from the college kid age.

I have already hinted to this fellow whose car I'm going to drive* that I thought I might interest the movies in an airplane movie (you see, Mom, we both got the same idea–must come from the same stock) and he even had this idea himself for after the war. I have not had a chance to go into detail with him on the subject. I'll also ask him about an inexpensive place to live. Don't worry about me being ashamed to say anything. Money or position never did dazzle me and never shall.

By the way there is a fellow on the post here who seems to like me. He proposed a couple of times anyway. His name is Gilbert, he comes from Massachusetts. I don't think I love him. At any rate, I do not know him well enough to marry him. Don't worry. I'll always let you know my plans. He is a load of fun and a nice guy. He is also absolutely nuts about flying (like me).

Love to all,
B.

*Lieutenant Bill Frentz, a fellow pilot at Pecos, wanted his car driven back to California where his mother and step-father live. I volunteered to do this for him since I want to go to California.

December 10, 1944

Dear Mom,

Friday I went to El Paso with another WASP, Lorraine Nelson and Saturday we went to Juarez where I spent all the money I had with me and still did not get enough gifts. I intended to buy only presents but this gal and I saw lots of good whiskey and so each bought four bottles to take back to Pecos and sell at a profit. Don't you think that's good? We spent $6 for a fifth and plan to sell it for $10.

I received word today from that fellow whose car I am supposed to drive, that he is getting a fourteen day leave starting the 20th and so will drive his own car out but he is going to take any of us who want to go to California and promises a nice Christmas in Los Angeles for all of us. I'm all set to get rolling on the 20th. I have a million things yet to do.

Just to keep us straight, so you won't worry I'll tell you how much money I have. Bank balance to date–$307. I had to draw checks from time to time to live on. November paycheck–$190 in my pocketbook. I shall need some cash and so will not deposit this check. There are still a few things to be paid for before leaving the post so I'll probably breeze right through the check. Am enclosing two war bonds.

Love to all,<br>B.

December 16, 1944

Dearest Mom and Dad,

How can I possibly thank you enough for your too good but very apropos gift. You really should not have given me so large a check. I wish I could somehow make all of this up to you. Here I have been away from home for almost a year and not contributing a cent. That is not bad enough, but you are always spending money on me–buying clothes, sending food, etc.

Hey, how does Alaska sound to you guys besides cold? I can get a job there as a radio operator for about $2,500 per annum but I want to think about it for a while. It would be lonely up there at a radio range station.

I am leaving here sometime on Wednesday by car. Bill Frentz is the name of the guy who is taking this other girl Peg Godfrey and me. He is very sweet. I believe I wrote to you about him before. You know what he did? He had his mother rent us a room in their apartment-hotel for the first couple of days we are there and until we find something. He says it will be hard for us to find a place.

I am going to keep a winter slack suit and buy a summer one. I am also going to buy my leather flying jacket and a couple of other incidentals that will all amount to between $25 and $35.

Time flies and I sure am not getting younger.* Strange though, I still feel very young and full of life and energy.

My best love to you all and again thank you so very much.

Love and kisses,<br>Bernice

*I had just celebrated my 24th birthday December 15, 1944

*Taken before a B-25. Standing: Peg Jamece Paxson, Shirley Phelps, Irene Norris, Joan Smythe, Mary MacLeod, Beverly Olson, Norma Sisler. Squatting: Margaret Godfrey, Mary Retick, Lorraine Nelson, Irene Crum, Ava Hamm, Bee Falk*

NOTE: This picture was used when I was on "To Tell the Truth" TV show taped November 9, 1977, for NBC-TV.

December 7, 1944, anniversary of Pearl Harbor–address by General H. H. Arnold, Commanding General, Army Air Force, before Class 44-10, the last class of WASP to graduate from Sweetwater, Texas:

"I am glad to be here today and talk with you young women who have been making aviation history. You and all WASP have been pioneers in a new field of wartime service and I sincerely appreciate the splendid job you have done for the Army Air Force. You, and more than nine hundred of your sisters, have shown that you can fly wingtip to wingtip with your brothers. If ever there were a doubt in anyone's mind that women can become skillful pilots, the WASP have dispelled that doubt.

The possibility of using women to pilot military aircraft was first considered in the summer of 1941. We anticipated then that global war would require all our qualified men and many of our women. We did not know how many of our young men could qualify to pilot the thousands of aircraft that American industry could produce. There was also the problem of finding sufficient highly capable young men to satisfy the demands of the Navy, the Ground Forces, the Service Forces and the Merchant Marine. England and Russia had been forced to use women to fly trainers and combat-type aircraft. Russian women were being used in combat.

In that emergency I called in Jacqueline Cochran, who had herself flown almost everything with wings and several times had won air races from men who now are general officers of the Air Forces. I asked her to draw up a plan for the training and use of American women pilots. She presented such a plan in late 1941 and it formed the basis for the Air Forces use of WASP.

Frankly, I didn't know in 1941 whether a slip of a young girl could fight the controls of a B-17 in the heavy weather they would naturally encounter in operational flying. Those of us who had been flying for twenty or thirty years knew that flying an airplane was something you do not learn overnight. But Miss Cochran said that carefully selected young women could be trained to fly our combat-type planes. So, it was only right that we take advantage of every skill that we, as a nation, possessed.

My objectives in forming the WASP were, as you know, three:

1. To see if women could serve as military pilots and, if so, to form the nucleus of an organization which could be rapidly expanded.

2. To release male pilots for combat.

3. To decrease the Air Forces' total demands for the cream of the manpower pool.

Well, now in 1944, more than two years since WASP first started flying with the Air Forces, we can come to only one conclusion–the entire operation has been a success. It is on the record that women can fly as well as men. In training, in safety, in operations, your showing is comparable to the over-all record of the Army Air Force flying within the continental United States. That is what you were called upon to do–continental flying. If the need had developed for women to fly our aircraft overseas, I feel certain that the WASP would have performed that job equally well. Certainly we haven't been able to build an airplane you can't handle. From AT-6s to B-29s, you have flown them around like veterans. One of the WASP has even test-flown our new jet plane.

You have worked hard at your jobs. Commendations from the generals to whose commands you have been assigned are constantly coming across my desk. These commendations record how you have buckled down to the monotonous, the routine jobs that are not much desired by our hot-shot young men headed toward combat or just back from an overseas tour. In some of your jobs I think they like you better than men.

I want to stress how valuable I believe this whole WASP program has been for the country. If another national emergency arises–let us hope it does not, but let us this time face the possibility–if it does, we will not again look upon a women's flying organization as experimental. We will know that they can handle our fastest fighters, our heaviest bombers; we will know that they are capable of ferrying, target towing, flying training, test flying and the countless other activities which you have proved you can do. This is valuable knowledge for the air age into which we are now entering. But please understand that I do not look upon the WASP and the job they have done in this war as a project or an experiment. A pioneering venture–yes; solely an experiment–no. The WASP are an accomplishment.

We are winning the war–we still have a long way to go–but we are winning it. Every WASP who has contributed to the training and operation of the Air Force has filled a vital and necessary place in the jigsaw pattern of victory. Some of you are discouraged, sometimes all of us are, but be assured you have filled a necessary place in the overall picture of the Air Forces.

The WASP have completed their mission. Their job has been successful. But, as is usual in war, it has not been without cost. Thirty-seven* WASP have died while helping their Country move toward the moment of final victory. The Air Force will long remember their service and their final sacrifice.

So, on this last graduation day, I salute you and all WASP. We of the Army Air Force are proud of you. We will never forget our debt to you."

**\* Actually, there were 38 who died.**

# NINE

# RETURN TO CIVILIAN LIFE

## Our trip to California

December 24, 1944

Dearest Mom,

We arrived safely after 24 hours of driving. Had a very uneventful and pleasant trip all the way out. There were four of us–Peggy Godfrey, WASP, Lieutenant. William Frentz (owner of the car) and Lieutenant Fox. We took turns driving and sleeping. The boys wouldn't let us pay for a thing not even our meals.

When we arrived here Bill Frentz had arranged with his mother for a room for Peg and me for five days (until we got settled) in the Gaylord Apartment Hotel where they live. They don't want us to pay a cent but we are trying now to see if we can at least pay for the room. You see Bill and Mr. and Mrs. Stavers (he is Bill's stepdad) have been taking Peg and me out every day and night to see the town. We have eaten at all the BEST (and I do mean BEST and fabulously expensive) places. We have been frequenting the hangouts of the movie stars and have seen loads of them.

In two days, here are some of the places we have gone to:

| | |
|---|---|
| Mocambo | The Tropics |
| George Murphy's | Swanee Inn |
| Romanoff's | Brown Derby |
| Beverly Hills Hotel–cocktail lounge | Lucey's |
| Wilshire Hotel–cocktail lounge | Ciro's |

Believe me they have spent a small fortune on us. Yesterday Peg and I bought Mrs. Stavers a pair of beach clappers (shoes) in Saks. She just wishes she had a large house so she could keep us with her. I also gave her a box of Barracinni's candy.

This morning I sneaked away early and found a place to stay starting tomorrow. It is Lacy Manor, 1619 West Olympic Boulevard, Los Angeles, California. It is $7 a week and reminds me very much of our house in Montclair. The woman who runs it (Mrs. Lacy) has a son in the Air Force and caters mostly to officers in service and to women and wives of servicemen. She does not take in just anyone and I will be sharing a room with two other girls and have access to the living room. She is a very sweet woman and tries to arrange little parties for everyone who comes in, if they have nothing to do. As a matter of fact, that is what she was doing while I was there.

Mrs. Stavers wants us to keep in close contact with her during our whole stay here. She said something to Bill about our coming to stay in their apartment with her about the 5th of January when her husband goes east for a while. I don't think I should do this though.

And now about the job situation. I intend to start searching Tuesday for an unusual position with good salary. If I don't find such a thing, I am going to come home. You see Los Angeles is so vast, so full of people all looking for a break, it would be silly for me to stay here with that in mind. I think I could do ten times better by getting just an ordinary job in New York. If I could just sit around with all the hoi polloi and belong to their clubs I might stand a chance here, but let's be honest with ourselves–you know Los Angeles–there are good opportunities for just a very few. And believe me living conditions are horribly expensive and impossible without a car. Nevertheless, I shall just fish around for a while and see what there is to see. At least I am getting to see Los Angeles, even though I don't know where I am half the time.

At any rate, Mom, don't worry. I am enjoying myself and am in good hands. You would love Mrs. Stavers. She reminds me so much of you.         Will write again soon.
                Love to all,
                    Bernice


                                        December 30, 1944
Dearest Mom,
    Well the kid will soon be on her way home. I can hear you saying it now, *I knew she would come home.* It is a long, long story and I hope you don't think me a failure or feel I have given up. You see I have given the

whole situation a lot of thought and also have been going all over the place (difficult in Los Angeles without a car as you know) and find that I can get a really good paying job but not a flying one. However, I can also get a good secretarial position at home and be able to save much more money so why not? Anyway there are millions of angles to the situation that I want to discuss with you.

Bill Frentz is going to drive back to Pecos Wednesday, January 3rd and will take me with him. I'll go as far as El Paso and from there try to hitch a ride on Army aircraft home. Do not worry about me since I shall be en route for an indefinite period. I want to stop at Fort Worth to see about a job as aircraft accident analyst that I applied for. They will be taking twelve WASP and probably have hundreds of applicants. If I stop in to see them, it might help me get the job. At any rate, if I can travel by military aircraft it won't hurt to stop in. Would also like to get to Washington, D.C. and visit Jacqueline Cochran who is in the hospital. She hears of jobs from time to time and again the person to person contact might work. I may be on my way for several days.

To say I am sorry I came to Los Angeles would be wrong because I am not. I have probably seen more of the place in a short period of time than does the every day tourist, thanks to Bill and his family. I have also spent very little money. But then this will take hours of relating, so be prepared to have your ears chewed off when I come home.

By the way, I sold all the whiskey I got in Juarez but only made $1.25 on each bottle. I'll sign off and be seeing you soon.

      Love and Kisses to all,
        Bernice


NOTE: During my stay in Los Angeles, I visited four movie studios trying to convince them they should make a movie about the WASP. While they were all very polite, none of them agreed to do this. One studio told me I should write a script and submit it. Since writing was not my expertise, I didn't undertake the project. Details of this follow in my January 7, 1945, letter to Lloyd.

I drove back to Pecos with Bill Frentz. From there I took a train to Fort Worth and went to the headquarters of the Army Air Force to learn what jobs might be available to the WASP–also in my letter to Lloyd. I then attempted to get a ride on an Army plane to New Jersey. For one month after we were disbanded, we were given permission to try for Air Force transportation. It was up to the pilot whether or not he would take us. I met a pilot who was going to New Jersey and in our discussion he made it clear to me what he expected me to do for him if he gave me a ride. It involved spending the night with him. I said "Thanks, but no thanks" and found someone else who was going to Buffalo, New York. I flew there and then took a train to Newark, New Jersey. When I arrived home there were letters from Lloyd that had been forwarded.


## From Lloyd in France

November 12, 1944

Dear Bernice,

It really is a shame. After all the work–physical and mental–you put into that course–and then you get the gate. As you say, in a way it indicates the cutting down on military personnel, which will mean the beginning of the reconversion. But still it is a shame. Nevertheless, I am sure that you do not consider it time wasted. You received training for nothing that you could not possibly have paid for on your own. And I am sure, if I know my sister, you will find something in the way of flying.

Now you know some of the advantages of living on an Army Post– especially on an almost officer status. In reality it is really an easy-going life. All the necessities of life are there. Here it is somewhat the same– except for a few of the necessities of life–namely heat. We are short on coal and wood. Consequently we now have one fire in a stove in one room, which we use as sort of a day room. It really isn't bad. But, oh, how I hate to get out of bed.

Our schedule is much easier now and I hope that we can keep it that way. I have not been to Paris of late. It is off limits. There really has not been much to do in the way of entertainment–unless you consider getting 'stonkin from dronkin' entertainment. Don't get me wrong. It is– but one cannot do this every night. We receive (or have up to now since being in France) a ration of four bottles of liquor, three scotch and one gin a month. In addition I have accumulated two or four bottles of champagne, a couple of cognac, benedictine, cointreau, etc. The Officer's Club here has a very interesting drink that they have concocted and call a boxcar. One third champagne, one third cognac, one third cointreau. One is enough to start an evening. Two to make it very enjoyable. Three to make any party a riot and four or five to end it–dead or otherwise. Have not tried the mixture yet–but I know the effects of each–and, well, you know.

Night before last several officers went to a gala Armistice Day celebration at a nearby village at the invitation of the local F.F.I. So naturally, who am I to stay home. And it was expected to be quite an affair –it started at 10 p.m. and the orchestra and stage show did not show up until 12. Frankly I never saw so much champagne in one place at one time. Literally–bottles by the hundred. A captain and I left at about 5 a.m.

Love,
Lloyd

## From Lloyd in France

December 15, 1944

Dear Bernice,

Happy Birthday, Keed, and on your next one we shall celebrate it together–I hope.

What have I been doing of late beside the usual? Well, haunting the opera in Paris. Call me Phantom of the Opera for short. Have seen altogether two ballets and about four operas–also a swell orchestral concert of Beethoven. These French orchestras are so very much better than those of London, there is no comparison. The ballets were swell too. But the opera is not heated (as are few of the buildings in Paris) and I don't see how they can stand around in those ballet costumes. They tell me the Follies-Bergère will close soon because it is too cold for the–ahem–statues.

Loads of Love,
Lloyd

## My Letter to Lloyd

January 7, 1945

Dear Lloyd,

I guess you have been wondering whether or not your sister had a permanent case of the writers' cramp or what have you.

Well, frankly, I have not but instead have been leaping around the country with my tail between my legs and licking my wounds. Truly getting de-armied is a horrible and unhappy problem for me. Believe me, here is one understanding soul to whom you can unburden yourself once they let you out. Perhaps you are laughing to yourself at this point and saying, *This kid won't suffer.* But just you wait and see what a problem it is to become civilized again.

To present a few facts, let me start from December 20th–THE day. I got a ride with a Lieutenant Frentz in his car plus another lieutenant and another WASP to Los Angeles. Lieutenant Frentz is of the wealthy variety with a wonderful mother and swell stepdad who reserved a room for us at the Gaylord for a few days and would not let us pay a cent. Then he proceeded to show WASP Godfrey and me most of the sights to be seen in Los Angeles.

In three days and two nights we hit many of the well-known spots too numerous to mention. They included Ciro's, The Macambo, Brown Derby, Lucey's, Romanoffs, Beverly Hills Hotel–cocktail lounge, Beverly Wilshire Hotel–cocktail lounge, Hollywood Bowl, Beverly Hills, the Pacific Ocean, etc.

It was sunny and lovely in Los Angeles but too cold for swimming. Just between you and me, I do not care too much for Los Angeles unless I could live there with oodles of do-re-mi. There is so much beauty and wealth in them thar hills that unless I could live that sort of life I fear I would be eaten up with jealousy. Perhaps that is just the sort of person I am. But actually after seeing all of that beauty and wealth I felt like a kid who had just devoured a one pound box of milk chocolate candy–not a stomachache but just too much. I wanted to get out in the middle of a desolate desert take a bath and wash off all the paint and then run through a green grassy field. (Didn't know you had a crazy sister–did you?)

Then I moved to a place more becoming to my means and proceeded on my own to see what the 'Big City' had to offer me that no other part of the country could. Want ads offered, or rather cried, for good secretaries at salaries beyond my wildest dreams a few years ago. But I can probably get the same thing around New York and cut my living expenses considerably. Besides, how would this take me close to flying if not in flying itself? Lieutenant Frentz's father had dropped a casual statement that often movie producers could use technical advisers in the productions of their films. As you may have seen, they are producing many winged pictures these days.

My first day on the loose found me hopping buses and tracking down Leo the Lion. "How are you going to get into the studios?" was the frenzied cry of the stranger. This is pathetically simple for one in an odd blue uniform with wings and fancy calling cards that have to be used up somehow. So I trot up to a reception desk, look businesslike and ask, "Who is the head of production?" A startled female replies, "Mr. Have-a-Cabbage." "I want to see Mr. Have-a-Cabbage, please." A skeptical look and–"Does Mr. Have-a-Cabbage expect you?" "No, he does not but here is my card." At this point she is completely non-plussed and calls Mr. Have-a-Cabbage's secretary who then speaks to me over the phone and is probably thinking–*Who the hell is Bernice S. Falk, Woman Airforce Service Pilot?*–I tell her my matter is most secret and I cannot discuss it over the phone.

Rapidly, a pass is made out for me and off I go. I speak to secretaries and directors and production men, etc. and soon find myself trying to convince them they should make a picture about the WASP. So I did crash four movie studios, see two movie sets, chat with a couple of two-bit movie stars and have a lovely adventure. Still, no job, no picture on the WASP. A couple of places wanted me to write a story and submit it (at my own time and expense, of course) but I can't even complete a sentence without a couple or three commas missing.

I next focus my attention on Lockheed and find I can get a secretarial job very easily. But what has this to do with flying?

So when Bill Frentz calls and says he is going back to Pecos I pack my bags and leave the very lonely 'Big City'.

I drove back to Pecos and from thence a coach ticket on the falling apart Texas and Pacific. I stopped in to see the guys at Headquarters–Army Air Force, Fort Worth, Texas, to see if they have any ideas on how to neatly dispose of ailing WASP–and they have plenty. One is to become a Link instructor and the other to instruct in mechanics, radio or radar. The latter appeals. Me what ain't got no edumacation learning some mugs how to rip apart a cylinder head. And I would be on an Army air field near the mechanical things I love. Who knows? Maybe even a ride once in a while?

They mention three fields where instructors are needed, Keesler Field, Mississippi; Amarillo, Texas; and Chanute Field, Illinois. I chose Chanute because I could detour a bit and stop there on my way home. The heads dispatch a letter signed by all the generals in the Air Force and their cousins, sisters, brothers and aunts and I dash off with a carbon copy.

I just came from Chanute Field where they are sure with the proper training I could be a good instructor but it seems that Army Air Force Regulation–2,745 3/4 does not permit them to train civilians. At Fort Worth I was told all of these details were being arranged but Chanute Field seems to know nothing of this. Hence, from me, a letter back to Fort Worth and I shall go home and see what the East Coast has to offer.

As you have undoubtedly grasped from all of this, I have a very dis-arranged mind as to what to do. I want to find one little spot in this whole world for just me. It can't be any old thing and since I am not in love, cannot fall back on the 'duties of a woman'. The whole trouble is that for Another realization I have come to is that I like small open places–country, fresh air, blue sky, clean living, with a binge sprinkled in here and there, and all of that there sort of stuff.

Still another thing that scares me is this restlessness–this lack of homesickness that dutifully belongs to all nice young girls. Sure I want to see the folks again, but I know after I'm home for two weeks, I'll want to move on again. Perhaps all of this can be attributed to the fact that we were placed on our own wobbly legs at a tender age. One of the many mysteries of life I guess.

I imagine I sound rather bitter and ungrateful throughout this whole theme.  Please believe me when I say I am not.  I am anything but that.  In the past ten months I have had more adventures, made more friends and developed more new attitudes on life and travel than most people experience in a lifetime. Now I must conquer and find myself.

Please forgive all of this drivel but I had to talk to someone tonight and who better than my mostest favorite brother?  Besides, I want you to be amused by it all since it has brought me many laughs and few or no worries.

Promise to write me pages and pages about you and please don't send me to Overbrook* because I'm really not a violent case.  Do you need anything like cigarettes, etc.?  If you need cigarettes and gum, no can do unless I can get on an Army Post because in civilian life they are as scarce as a Hawaiian in the South Pole.

Please take care of yourself and tell "Ike"** to let you come home soon.  Believe it or not, I misses you-all.

Moocha Luff,
Bernice


\* An insane asylum in Caldwell, New Jersey.
\*\* General Dwight D. Eisenhower.

My mother always said "everything happens for the best".  She said this when we were disbanded and I decided this time my mother was wrong. In retrospect she was so correct.  Had I continued in the Army Air Corps, I would never have met my wonderful husband, Joe Haydu, and had 3 wonderful children.  So, again, mother was right.

# TEN

# NOW WHAT?

After the disbanding of the WASP December 20, 1944, and my trip to California, I returned to New Jersey. Early in 1945 I started practicing for my flight instructor's rating in East Stroudsburg, Pennsylvania, in a Piper J-3 Cub. I also studied for ground instructor's ratings in navigation, theory of flight, aircraft and engines. July 7th I took my Civil Aeronautics Administration flight instructor's test ride and passed.

Television was a thing of the future. These were the days when people were glued to their radios for news and entertainment. I thought it would be timely to have a radio program about flying and tried my hand at writing radio scripts for a program called "Wings Over New Jersey." Two stations were interested WNJR, Newark, and WPAT, Paterson. WJNR assigned a professional scriptwriter who wrote a sample program that was produced but we were unable to find a sponsor.

In 1945 the government started distributing surplus training aircraft around the United States and selling them to the general public at greatly reduced prices. These had to be delivered from Air Force bases to dealers. I learned who these dealers were and contacted them offering my services as a ferry pilot. I would take an airline or train to pick up the plane. Some of the military bases were in Augusta, Georgia; Ponca City, Oklahoma; Cape Girardeau, Missouri; and Union City, Tennessee. Most of the planes were delivered to Albany, New York and Somerset, New Jersey. I received a fee plus expenses for each trip. Sometimes I would go alone and sometimes as part of a group. I recall one time when the dealer wanted to send three of us for three aircraft. The other two were men who didn't want me to go with them since they had plans for themselves on the return trip that didn't include me. The dealer was reluctant to send me alone but I convinced him I could handle the trip solo, which I did.

The rest of 1945 I did both ferrying and flight instructing at Woodbridge Airport, Iselin, New Jersey. Flight instructors were paid $3.00 per hour.

Manufacturers of aircraft for private use were beginning production this year, as no civilian planes had been built since before the war. I contacted the distributors for Cessna and Aeronca asking if they could use a ferrying service to bring aircraft from the factory to La Guardia Airport, New York. The Cessna aircraft were manufactured in Wichita, Kansas and the Aeronca in Middletown, Ohio. There were times when many aircraft had to be delivered, so in addition to my ferrying, I hired others pilots. Many of them I selected from pilots returning from the military as well as some WASP in the area. I would check them out at Iselin Airport in the type of aircraft they would be flying and supply them with the proper charts for the trip. Sometimes we went as a group of four or five and sometimes I went alone. We took the train to Ohio and an airline to Wichita, Kansas.

The Cessna distributor for the Metropolitan area was pleased with my ability, service and efficiency in running the ferrying venture and offered me a dealership.

As an incentive to dealers, there was a sliding scale of commissions for the fiscal year. If you sold five aircraft you received 10% commission, another five you received an additional 5% retroactive through the first one sold, another five you received an additional 5% also retroactive. This incentive worked for me. In that fiscal year I sold twenty aircraft, which gave me a total of 20% on all the planes sold. They sold for between $3,000 and $4,000 each depending on the model and the equipment in the plane. I actually did not have the twentieth airplane sold but purchased it myself to obtain the full retroactive 20% commission.

I grossed over $12,000 that year. According to the Inflation Calculator $12,000 in 1946 is the equivalent of $115,500 in 2002.

As anyone who has sold 'cold turkey' knows, it is not easy. In this case, it was especially difficult, since the airplane had to be paid for in full when ordered–prior to delivery–sight unseen.

I would fly my demonstrator plane to small airports all over New Jersey attempting to sell flight schools, airport owners and operators as well as individuals. Sometimes I would hear of individuals wanting a plane but it was out of reach financially. I would introduce them and suggest they form a flight club. Meanwhile, I had written sample rules for club ownership, which they could modify for their use. That concept of shared ownership helped more people be able to afford a plane.

# The Eddie Accaro Episode.

One of the more interesting moments in my search for buyers was when I flew to Blairstown Airport, New Jersey, to demonstrate to the operator of the airport. That airport was famous for the adjoining hotel, which had a restaurant noted for its excellent food. Upon my arrival, I was told I would have to wait to see the operator, so I walked to the restaurant for lunch. Suddenly, I was paged and asked to come to the airport. There I was informed that when the line-boy (young men who did odd jobs around the airport, sometimes just to earn flight time) parked my aircraft he ran into the back of another Cessna of the same type, damaging the front of my aircraft and the back of the other.

The owner of that aircraft had also been paged and introduced himself. He was Eddie Accaro and he went on to tell me that he not only had a dangerous hobby but also a dangerous profession. The naïve person I was, I did not realize I was talking to the most famous jockey of that time, one who had won a record number of races. The airport operator arranged to fly us to our destinations. Accaro was such a fine gentleman that he authorized the operator to take the parts needed to repair my plane from his, knowing I needed my plane as a demonstrator.

While I was dating Joe Haydu, he owned racehorses. In one of the races the jockey on Joe's horse was–you guessed it–Eddie Accaro. And so our paths crossed once again.

*September 1950—Joe and Bee in the winning circle with Admiral's Tune, one of Joe's horses. The jockey was L. Batcheller. How about the way we dressed in those days?*

Financial, Insurance
Real Estate

# NEWARK SUNDAY CALL

Editorial Page
Gardens, Photography

PART
IV

NEWARK, N. J., SUNDAY, AUGUST 18, 1946.

## Orange Girl Heads Plane-Ferrying Company—and Flys 'Em, Too

Bernice Falk of East Orange, head of Garden
State Airways, goes over a route with two of
her pilots, Bob Donnelly, left, and George
Fuchs, before starting ferry trip. Company flies
new light planes from manufacturer to dealer.

George Fuchs greets Miss Falk on
arrival at Somerset Hills with new
Cessna which she flew across country
from factory.

### Excerpts from the August 18, 1946, *Newark Sunday Call*

" 'A girl who wants to make a career out of aviation has one strike against her before she starts–she's a girl.' Miss Falk said yesterday. 'Even though the planes are carefully inspected before we take them, since they are brand new, there is always a chance of some little thing going wrong.' Just the other week Bee got drenched with gasoline shortly after takeoff. The fuel indicator had worked loose and was spraying gas around the cockpit. She pulled out a nail file and with a couple of deft twists, stopped the leak. …This young flyer has found out how to get along with male pilots, a group noted for its implicit belief in the superiority of the male when it comes to flying. 'A girl should never, never brag about her flying before men. Sometimes it is even better to play a little helpless and stupid.' …Ferry trips are only made when the forecast calls for good flying conditions. One reason for this is that most of the ferry routes cross the Allegheny Mountains–'rough' flying country even under ideal conditions."

**PLANE FERRY**

# *She flies and still pounds typewriter!*

*FLYING TRIO--Pilot Bob Sauer of Basking Ridge, right, points to an overcast sky, while pilots Bernice Falk of East Orange, and Arthur Martone of Harrison, wonder when the "soup" will clear up over Somerset Hills Airport. Miss Falk is founder and Chief Executive of Garden State Airways.*

Excerpts from the December 22, 1946, *Sunday Star Ledger*

"Flying duties take Miss Falk and her staff of broad shouldered ex-combat pilots all over the country…Miss Falk, who is rated one of the best light plane pilots in the state, got the idea for her ferrying concern as a result of a job she held down shortly after the war, ferrying surplus Army planes to disposal points throughout the country. The topography of the country is as familiar to Miss Falk as the palm of her hand. 'The Rocky Mountains are pretty, but bare, although some peaks are snowcapped. However, the Alleghenies though lower, are more dangerous to fly over,' she says, 'because of turbulent air currents.' She recalls that once while flying over Pennsylvania, near Altoona, she hit an unexpectedly vicious down draft. 'The plane dropped 1,000 feet in 30 seconds. The plane fell from under me so quickly that if I hadn't had my safety belt fastened, I would have burst through the cowl.' Had she been over a ridge at the time, she would have crashed a very valuable plane she was delivering to a New York buyer. The fact that she was over a valley saved her. The plane had enough leeway so that its forward speed could pull it out of the downdraft."

# Girl Flyer And Former WASP Discovers Selling Airplanes Ideal Business For Her

*PILOT AND SALESWOMAN--Miss Bernice S. Falk, flight instructor and saleswoman, looks over a plane preparatory to either flying it, or giving a sales talk on its fine points. She uses her vocation, flying, in the unusual business of operating an airplane sales agency.*

Excerpts from the January 9, 1947, *East Orange Record*

"Convinced that a woman had to make her own place in aviation because of the prejudice against her as pilot, Miss Falk decided to get her instructor's rating and teach students to fly. She explained that many women do make as good pilots as men but that it is difficult for them to overcome the doubts and fears of the public and commercial airlines. .. As an instructor she still encountered a few students who did not want to fly with a woman. However, she explained that the fears of 'doubting Thomases' could be overcome by having them watch the progress of her other students."

Part Owner of Flight School

My Cessna demonstrator was in a hangar at Woodbridge Airport, Iselin, New Jersey, where I also  instructed.  The owner/operator was James Ruscoe trading as Ruscoe Flying Service.  He wanted to sell his flight school, which had many World War II veterans as students.

After the war a veteran could attend college, or other schools including flight schools, for which the Government paid tuition up to a certain amount under the G.I. Bill of Rights. Ruscoe had many of these students. Jim approached a group of us offering to sell his business for $28,000. There were nine of us willing to purchase. I paid for my share by giving the corporation my Cessna demonstrator. Some of the nine were to be active in the operation while others preferred to remain as silent partners. My job was to instruct as well as to keep the books and help with operations. This left me no time to continue with the Cessna dealership.

*Ruscoe Flying Service–Pictured standing Steve Galaida,\* Lou Seaburg, Don O'Connell, Walter Kavonetz, Carl Rasmussen,\* Bill Gilgannon, Jim Stine.\* Squatting: Jim Ruscoe, Dick Williams,\* Bernice Falk,\*Ed Carr,\* Erwin Whittmore*
*\* 6 of the 9 owners of Ruscoe Flying Service*

<u>Excerpts from the November 25, 1946</u>
<u>New Brunswick, New Jersey, Newspaper</u>

### 8,000 WITNESS FIRST POST-WAR
### AIR SHOW AT WOODBRIDGE FIELD

"Program, sponsored by New Veterans' Flying Club, presented for big crowd at Iselin:

A PT-19\* aircraft piloted by Matt E. Gil performed a series of slow rolls, inverted flying and other acrobatic maneuvers.

Dick Williams, chief instructor, did a series of spins and landed dead-stick\*\* in an Aeronca Champion.

Army Reserve pilots from Newark Airport flew formation in P-51 aircraft.

There was more formation flying in Aeronca Champions.

Balloon-bursting and spot landing contests were held. ***

Miss Bernice Falk struck a humorous note in the afternoon's program when she skillfully put on a comedy act in an Aeronca Champion. The flyer, who served with the WASP during the war, appeared dressed as an 'old lady' for her first 'hour of instruction'. Without waiting for an instructor, however, the 'old lady' climbed into the cockpit and took off in a wobbly fashion. After that she kept the crowd well entertained with several attempts at landing. ****

Sherwood Cole was scheduled to close the show with a parachute jump but because of the unexpectedly large crowd it was decided it was too risky with little space left to land due to the large number of people and cars."

* Aircraft had these designations:

|  |  |
|---|---|
| PT–Primary Trainer | BT–Basic Trainer |
| AT–Advanced Trainer | P–Pursuit |
| B–Bomber | A–Attack |

** At an altitude the pilot feels he can safely land he turns off the engine and the plane, in effect, becomes a glider. This requires a great deal of control and skill.

*** Large balloons are released and the plane while flying tries to burst them. For spot landings, a section of the runway is designated with lines and the plane attempts to land between the two lines.

**** Those of you who have attended air shows may have seen similar stunts performed.

*Bernice Falk as an 'old lady' after performing at the air show.*

# Demise of the Flight School

The Garden State Parkway, a major highway in New Jersey, was in the process of being constructed. The path of the highway took the end off one of our runways. On December 12, 1947, we were notified by the Civil Aeronautics Administration that the airport no longer met their requirements or those of the State Aviation Department (now the Federal Aviation Administration). We were forced to move our operation to nearby Hadley Airport. Since there was another flight school at Hadley we had to agree that we would not solicit new students. On June 30, 1948, our license with the government for students under the G. I. Bill of Rights expired because we had no permanent field from which to operate.

We retained an attorney who advised us to visit the governor wearing our uniforms as veterans of World War II and tell him how we were being treated. Since we rented the airport and were not owners of the land, we had little legal standing. Mr. Ransford J. Abbott, executive assistant to Governor Alfred Driscoll, interviewed us and promised to try to have our problem resolved as quickly as possible. The partners elected me to be the spokesperson. This entailed about twenty-five trips to the State Aviation Highway Department and the governor's office in Trenton. There were conferences with our attorney in Jersey City who had advised us to say we had no legal representation because of the cost.

The strategy worked! The case against the New Jersey Department of Transportation was finally settled towards the end of 1948 with each of the owners of the flight school receiving the share of the $28,000 they had invested. We were never told how much Mr. Shinn, the owner of the airport received but we did hear that at one point he had turned down $44,000. We invited Mr. Shinn to join us in hiring an attorney but he refused knowing we were already doing all the work that should have been his. After the settlement, for which we had worked so hard, he took us out for an ice cream soda!!!

Once we had settled with the State of New Jersey, we disbanded the corporation.

# Now What?–Again!

Again, I was faced with trying to get a job involving aviation and flying. *The New York Times* want ads revealed one that had some appeal. True, it was an office job but it did require someone with extensive knowledge. The office was located on 42nd Street in New York City. I was interviewed by Richard T. Adams, a partner in Indamer Corporation (India and America). Peter Baldwin, the other partner, was in India. My job as executive secretary was to procure and properly ship aircraft and parts to India. There were four of us in the office. Although much paper work was involved, one compensating factor was that the company owned a Beechcraft Bonanza, which I was allowed to fly on my own time. I held this job until the end of 1950.

While working there, I had a very scary experience. In July 1949 I was to visit a business contact in Connecticut. Our offices were just a few blocks from Grand Central Station. It was a very hot day and I was late and had to run to catch the train. The train was air conditioned and exceptionally cold and I was hot and perspiring from running. When I reached my destination and started talking my voice felt very strained. A few days later I was treated for what appeared to be laryngitis. My condition worsened and by August my right vocal chord was paralyzed and my voice was 'husky'. The first doctor I visited told me the left vocal chord would compensate and I would just have a 'sexy' low-pitched voice from then on. By October my left vocal cord was also paralyzed leaving me with an almost complete loss of voice.

Altogether, I visited seven doctors, each an expert in his field, but none could determine what had caused the paralysis. While suffering from laryngitis and unable to speak I would find it necessary to write down my questions to people. Invariably the answer was shouted at me. They assumed that since I was 'dumb' I was also deaf. I found myself walking in the shoes of those with disabilities and I learned to empathize with them.

By November, slight movement of the left cord was observed and within two months my voice was once again normal with the exception of my singing. I used to have a good singing voice but that was gone. Small price to pay.

During that time, Joe and I were dating on a regular basis. He took me up in his airplane to a high altitude and did some wild maneuvers thinking it might help. It did not but it showed me the wonderful character of this man who never deserted me in my time of need.

I resigned to marry Joseph Haydu in 1951. He was old fashioned and did not want his wife working. But he was modern enough that he owned a plane and thought it was wonderful that she shared his love for flying and that they could fly together.

**Obviously, a match made in heaven!**

# ELEVEN

# MARRIAGE AND CHILDREN

While I was still involved with the flight school in Iselin, New Jersey, I met Joseph Haydu. He was the President and in today's jargon CEO of S. Haydu & Sons, the largest independent meat processor in New Jersey. Joe had been a flight instructor in World War II for three and a half years. His hobby was flying and he owned a Stagger Wing Beechcraft.

I had been invited to do a radio interview by a station in Jersey City, New Jersey. The people conducting the interview lived in East Orange, where I lived and they offered to give me a ride to the station. Joe was to be interviewed two weeks later and they asked him to come to the studio that night to discuss his up-coming program.

### This is where we met.

I had heard of this handsome, wealthy Joe Haydu and as is the case when you hear so many wonderful things about a person, you feel you may be disappointed when meeting. I was definitely not disappointed!

I learned later that one day when Joe was at the Basking Ridge Airport he had seen me fly in. I was purchasing fuel for a Cessna I was delivering to Long Island. After I took off, Joe asked, "Who was that attractive woman pilot?" He too was not disappointed.

After the discussion of his radio interview was completed, Joe invited all of us out for a drink. When ready to leave the lounge he asked me if he could take me home. Teasingly, I said, "Will it be safe?" Teasingly, he replied, "No." So I refused. However, the next evening he phoned and formally asked for a date. Our first date was on Valentine's Day. ( I still have the blouse I wore on that date some fifty-five years ago). We went to the Log Cabin, a popular nightclub, where they had a live band.

*Joe and Bee*

In those days the big bands– Benny Goodman, Glen Miller, Harry James, Jimmy and Tommy Dorsey, Les Brown and his 'Band of Renown', to name a few, gave live performances across the country at popular nightclubs. Some of the popular singers with the bands were Frank Sinatra, Peggy Lee, Doris Day, Helen O'Connell, Bob and Ray Eberly, Perry Como, and many others. Saturday night dates usually involved

*Joe and Bee with Stevey 2, Joey 3, Diana 1.*

attending one of these places and dancing until the wee hours. Joe was a good dancer–a plus in my book. During the evening he said, "I'm going to marry you." I thought, *This guy has quite a line.*

We were married February 28, 1951. It would have been sooner but we had a problem to resolve concerning the fact we were of different religions. Joe is Presbyterian and I am Jewish. Neither one of us would consider asking the other to convert. We finally resolved the situation by agreeing to raise our children in the Unitarian faith. Our religious differences have never been a problem. We each respect the preferences of the other.

The first years of our marriage were filled with the pleasures of young children.

July 3, 1952–Joseph Daniel (Joey).

November 25, 1953–Steven Charles (Stevey).

December 17, 1954–Diana Bernice.

At one point we had three in diapers!

This never bothered me since I knew that if they were not rapidly potty trained, by the time they reached the age of twenty-one they would be able to change their own diapers. Because of these responsibilities as well as Joe's involvement with expanding his business we sold the Stagger Wing Beech and attended to the practical side of living.

It was not until March 1964 that we went back to flying. A friend of ours Calvin Theobald kept his four-seater Cessna 172 N9831T at Totowa-Wayne Airport in New Jersey. (All aircraft have a certificate number beginning with the letter N to which they refer in radio transmissions.) Calvin asked us if we wanted to fly his airplane to which we readily agreed. He offered me his plane to use in any race I would like to enter.

## We were off and flying again.

In June 1964 we purchased a beautifully restored PT-17 Stearman N179M, which won first prize as best restored aircraft at Blairstown Airport, New Jersey, in July 1964; Caldwell Airport, New Jersey, September 1964; and the Reading Pennsylvania Air Show in June 1966.

*Joe and Bee Haydu in their Stearman, Stevey and Diana each holding a trophy won at air shows, Joey on the wing. This picture was included in the article by Jack Elliott.*

Excerpts from the December 20, 1964, *Sunday Star Ledger*

## HUSBAND, WIFE FIND RELAXATION IN WILD BLUE YONDER

"For relaxation, Joe Haydu of Livingston likes to don his parachute, helmet and goggles and take his Stearman biplane upstairs to do a few loops and rolls and spins. And what do you suppose Joe's wife, Bee, likes to do for relaxation? She likes nothing better than to don a parachute, helmet and goggles and take the Stearman upstairs to do a few loops and rolls and spins…Stearman 179M, which is based at Totowa-Wayne Airport, was built in 1943. It has been perfectly restored and now wears its original colors, blue and yellow, with the stars on the wings and the old striped tail. It looks like it just came out of the factory. …Flying in something like 179M is something entirely apart from flying in today's plush, modern aircraft. This is real, old-fashioned flying. You climb into a parachute (a piece of equipment the modern pilot is unfamiliar with) before you climb into the cockpit. And you don a helmet and goggles because you're sitting out in the open. We went for a ride in 179M a few weeks ago, with Joe at the controls. He did a spin, a loop, an Immelmann turn, and a half roll so we could get the feel of hanging on the strap and looking at the sky below and the ground above. Man, that's flying!"

The Stearman was a wonderful family plane. We loved  taking relatives and friends for airplane rides.  Joe had been attempting to teach me a routine that I could use in an air show should the occasion arise. It consisted of doing a series of spins culminating in a loop out of which I was to land. In November 1964 we had invited our friends, Gerry and Madeline Gilligan, and their six children for rides in our Stearman. I was to take Gerry for a ride in 179M. Before taking off, I asked him if he had ever done any acrobatics and if he would like to. His answer was in the affirmative so I flew the routine with him. The next day when Joe took our son Joey flying, Joey held up the seat belt which had come loose from its mooring. Joe related this to Gerry and told him there had been a good possibility he could have fallen out of the open cockpit airplane, in which case he would have had to use the parachute–we always wore one in that plane. Gerry's reply was, "Oh, no, I would never have fallen out because I was holding on to the sides of that cockpit so tight I would have taken the airplane with me."

One of the most delightful experiences for me was in October 1964 when I flew my mother to Rockland, Maine, in the Cessna 172 to meet some friends. One woman was over ninety and had never been in an airplane. We convinced her she should have this adventure. While flying and making a turn, she nervously tapped me on the shoulder and quietly said, "Did you know, dear, your wing is down?" She didn't realize that when making a turn the wing dips in the direction of the turn.

Our children were privileged to be able to try their hands at flying when they were quite young. As soon as they were old enough we arranged for them to have flying lessons in addition to giving them some ourselves. Although none of them has made flying a profession, they have enjoyed experiencing the marvels and beauty of the skies and have delighted in the knowledge gained while learning to soar above the earth at a young and impressionable age. Steve did continue flying for pleasure.

## Flying with Jacqueline Cochran

Years had gone by and most of the WASP were busy rearing families. We had lost touch. One of the WASP Marty Wyall attempted to reactivate the group. She sent notices to those she could locate and called a meeting to coincide with a Ninety-Nines Convention (an international organization of licensed women pilots) in Cincinnati, Ohio, in August 1964. She invited Jacqueline Cochran to attend, which Jackie did.

After the meeting Ms. Cochran announced she had room in her multi-engine Lockheed Lodestar for anyone wanting to fly back to the New York area the next day. She piloted her own plane. I couldn't pass up such an opportunity. Once we were airborne, she asked if I were still flying. Since my answer was, "Yes", she invited me to copilot, and was gracious enough to sign my log book stating I had flown her N-13V Lodestar from Cincinnati, Ohio, to La Guardia Field, New York, for approximately three hours. She wrote me as follows:

Suite 34 K · The Waldorf Towers
100 East Fiftieth Street
New York, N.Y. 10022

September 17, 1964

TO WHOM IT MAY CONCERN:

This is to advise that Mrs. Bernice Falk Haydu flew my N-13V Lodestar from Cincinnati, Ohio, to La Guardia Field, New York City. The approximate flying time was three hours.

*Jacqueline Cochran*
JACQUELINE COCHRAN

*Cochran's Letters*

Suite 34 K · The Waldorf Towers
100 East Fiftieth Street
New York, N.Y. 10022

September 17, 1964

Dear Mrs. Haydu:

Thank you for your very nice letter of August 17th. It was a real pleasure to attend the WASP Reunion in Cincinnati and see all the girls again.

I was very happy to have you and Miss Coakley on the return trip to New York, and I am enclosing statement of your flying time—you did a fine job as pilot.

I would love to play golf with you but we'll have to postpone our game until later as I leave for Europe on September 25th and will not return until the middle of November. Then I am off on a trip to Mexico until around the first of the year.

With kindest regards.

Sincerely yours,

*Jackie*
Jacqueline Cochran

Enc.

Mrs. Bernice Falk Haydu
22 Chestnut Street
Livingston, New Jersey

*Jacqueline Cochran was kind enough to send me this autographed picture. June 4, 1964, in this Lockheed she set 2 new women's speed records. 1,302 miles per hour for the 100 kilometer event and 1,135m.p.h. for the 500 kilometer course which follows her recent 1,429.297 m.p.h. record set for the 15/25 kilometer straight away event.*

Jackie was an avid golfer. As we flew over the country-side and saw golf courses stretching out below us she told me that one day when she was no longer able to fly she would like to play every golf course in the country. Joe and I had occasion to play golf with her twice at the 1969 WASP reunion in Indio, California. She was a good golfer, as one would expect. She applied herself diligently to whatever she undertook, which was the secret of her successes. She earned them. She was successful in being the first woman to break the sound barrier, she won more races and received more awards than any other woman flyer and I believe that honor still stands.

While playing golf with her in Indio, she pointed out the home of former president Dwight D. Eisenhower located on the golf course. She mentioned that if Mamie, Eisenhower's wife, were home, she would bring us a glass of iced tea. They were good friends. Jackie had given Dwight the use of a small cottage on her ranch for his personal office. I really liked Jackie. She was a very direct person, mincing no words. You always knew where you stood with her. She was also very aggressive, which is why she was able to accomplish as much as she did, including establishing the WASP.

In July and September 1964 we attended air shows at Blairstown Airport, and Caldwell Airport, New Jersey, displaying our Stearman PT-17. On both these occasions we won first place for best-restored aircraft.

Johnny Foyle, a well-known aerobatic pilot who performed at many air shows, asked if I would fly in formation with him around the area, to attract the attention of local residents, hoping they would be enticed to attend the air show. He too had a Stearman but his had a 450-horsepower engine, ours had 220-horsepower. I was flattered by the invitation but pointed out the difference in our horsepower. He said he would slow down and I should speed up. We did and it worked out fine, just as he said it would.

The following year, Johnny was in Miami, Florida attending an air show. He had been asked to fly his airplane in formation with another aircraft, an AT-6 (650-horsepower) so publicity pictures could be taken. Unfortunately, while in flight they collided. Johnny was killed.

In September 1965 The Prop 'N Wing Club had a Fly-In where trophies and awards were given. We had the distinction of being awarded Best Stearman Trophy on which is engraved:

**JOHNNY FOYLE MEMORIAL TROPHY**
**Outstanding Restoration Stearman Biplane**
**Awarded by A.L. Bachmann**

Al Bachmann was a famous air show announcer. We still remember Johnny and proudly display this trophy in our home.

In April 1966 we purchased a six seat, twin-engine Cessna 3101, N1015, which was more suitable for cross-country and enabled us to take more trips with the children. We flew to many air shows and took trips with the family to places such as Niagara Falls

*Joey (12), Joe, Bee, Stevey (11), Trophy on ground.*

and to Montauk Point, Long Island, where the beach was within walking distance of the airport. A regular trip was to Florida where we frequently vacationed in the winter and where we finally settled in our retirement.

## Link Trainer

We could always depend on Joe to come up with the unusual as he did in 1966. In World War II pilots were taught to fly under instrument conditions not only in the aircraft but also on the ground in a Link trainer. I described this earlier when talking about how we were given instrument training. Joe learned of a Link trainer for sale and, of course, he purchased it. Not to be deterred by the fact that we had no room for it, Joe had our back porch enlarged, enclosed and the ceiling raised to accommodate it. Our family and friends took turns 'flying' on our porch. We eventually donated it to the Civil Air Patrol.

### Excerpts from the January 8, 1967, *Sunday Star Ledger* Article by Jack Elliott

### PILOT'S GROUNDED...AND HE LIKES IT

"Sometimes when the weather is so miserable nobody in his right mind would think of going out of the house, Joe Haydu of Livingston will say to his wife, Bee, 'I think I'll do a little flying.'...What he is talking about is going out on the back porch and climbing into their Link trainer. Joe can lay

out a course, flip the switches and to all intents and purposes actually fly it. The Link even has a recorder to tell him how accurately he flew it."

### Other Things

Joey and some of his friends organized a band called The Changing Times. They were hired to play at parties and would practice in our backyard. We had a pool and gave frequent parties. Of course we always invited the neighbors, which is why they never complained about the band practices.

*Young Joey Haydu goes flying in his father's Link trainer as his mom gives encouragement.*

130

*Music was a part of our children's lives. We had a piano, an organ as well as a portable organ and an accordion. All three took lessons on the piano. Diana also played the accordion and the boys the organs. This picture was taken for inclusion in the July 9, 1967, issue of the Newark Sunday News when an article was written about the Powder Puff Derby, mentioned in chapter 12.*

## Penny-A-Pound Airlift

From time to time the Ninety-Nines, Inc. conduct a charity event entitled Penny-A-Pound Airlift. Rides in an airplane are given to women who pay one penny for each pound they weigh. The planes are flown by members of the Ninety-Nines and the proceeds benefit aerospace education and the Amelia Earhart Scholarship Fund.

In May 1968 I had the pleasure of chairing this function at Chatham Aviation, Morristown Municipal Airport, New Jersey, and was ably assisted by my daughter Diana and her friend, Monica Landusco. They were very excited about flying and planned to become members of the Civil Air Patrol. (An organization still in existence that encourages young people to take an interest in aviation.) The girls had a wonderful time helping by selling tickets, assisting people into the planes and cooking the hot dogs and hamburgers sold at the refreshment stand. In addition to the flying there were displays of many new and old aircraft as well as door prizes.

We received publicity from fourteen local newspapers and radio stations. This picture was in the May 16, 1968, West *Essex Tribune*, Livingston, New Jersey:

*MOMENTS OF TRUTH – Charlotte McCollum, left, of Hackettstown and Bee Haydu check the scale with daughter, Diana Haydu, Heritage Junior High student, in preparation for the Penny-A-Pound Airlift. Bee Haydu is chairman of the airlift, sponsored by the Ninety-Nines, Inc., a group of licensed women pilots.*

# Smithsonian Air and Space Museum

In 1969 during one of the school vacations we thought it would be nice to take the children to Washington, D.C. We were anxious to visit the Smithsonian Air and Space Museum where I was certain they must have quite a bit about the WASP. Much to my dismay there was no mention of the WASP anywhere in the museum. I was really angry. What surprised me most is that a quarter of a century had gone by and no one had noticed the omission–or if they had, no one had done anything about it. Joe, always one to encourage me, suggested I contact them. I spoke with Paul Garber, historian emeritus. He apologized for the lack of WASP coverage and asked if I had something to offer. Along with other items, I donated my dress uniform, which is still there on display. The dress uniform I now wear was given to me by WASP Gretchen Grabba who was dying of cancer and unable to participate in our efforts to be recognized as veterans of World War II. She said that she would feel a part of it if, as president of the WASP organization, I would wear her uniform to the many hearings and formal occasions. More about that later.

*AT SMITHSONIAN – Paul Garber, historian emeritus of the National Air and Space Museum, discusses WASP history with Bee Haydu of Livingston, dressed in WASP uniform while S. Paul Johnston, director of the museum looks on. They are standing in front of Wiley Post's "Winnie Mae" airplane.*

"Appropriately, Mrs. Haydu presented the material while standing before a very famous 'lady' in aviation history–the "Winnie Mae," globe-circling aircraft which Wiley Post flew in the first circumnavigation of the earth by air in 1931."

My children were really impressed that I could still fit into the uniform after twenty-five years. They thought it was 'pretty sharp' looking and could even be worn today. They were especially surprised that the skirt wasn't down to my ankles–actually it falls just below the knees because they were trying to save on fabric during the war.

## More About the Smithsonian

At the 1969 WASP reunion in Indio, California, Mrs. Leota "Dedie" Deaton who had been the Chief Staff Executive Officer in Sweetwater had a small suitcase filled with pictures that had been taken during our training. Knowing the Smithsonian did not have much about us, I asked Dedie if she would lend me her collection so I could take it to them for copying. I did this as well as convincing eight WASP from classes 43-1 through 43-8 to donate their wings, which were different from the final ones. Collectors pay a great deal for these authentic, unusual wings. It was not until the class of 44-1 that we were issued the wings with the diamond shaped shield. It is said this was selected because it was the shape of the shield carried by Athena, the goddess of wisdom, warfare and the practical arts. The Smithsonian now displays a complete collection.

About this time they were in the process of building a new building. On one of our visits to deliver items, Joe and I came in through the main entrance. As we looked to the left, we recognized the man on a scaffold painting a huge mural that went three stories high from floor to ceiling. It was Eric Sloane, the noted artist, writer and antique tool collector. He had donated his services, but complained to us that the only things he could deduct from his income tax were the paint and brushes–nothing for his labor. When you visit the Air and Space Museum, be sure to go in the main entrance and look to the left.

## The Story of Eric Sloane

Before we were married and while I had my Cessna dealership, I participated in a showroom aircraft display in New York City. It was at this show that I first saw and fell in love with Eric Sloane's cloud paintings. They were so realistic. I thought that someday I would like to own one. It was not until shortly after we were married and were looking for a painting to hang over a large sofa in our living room that I had occasion to come across some of Sloane's paintings again. We were dining with friends in a Long Island restaurant where some of Eric's paintings were on display. After some research, I located him in his studio in New York City. He invited Joe and me to a showing he was having at the Roosevelt Hotel. There we saw a very large painting he had been commissioned to do by Lockheed Aviation. It depicted an F-80 jet in front of beautiful cumulus clouds. We told him we liked a certain group of clouds in that painting and asked if he could duplicate them in the size we needed and if he would insert a small plane in the picture.

We invited him to our apartment, a third-floor walkup, in East Orange, New Jersey, for dinner so he could see where we intended to hang the painting. He accepted and asked if he could bring his dog, Nimbo, named after the cumulonimbus clouds. Upon his arrival, it turned out that the dog was a huge German shepherd and was so big and friendly we thought his wagging tail would knock everything off the coffee table. I am embarrassed to say that we gave Eric the dimensions we wanted and showed him where we intended to hang his painting. It was as if we were ordering some cabinetry for the kitchen. That didn't seem to bother him and he said he would contact us when it was finished. We also reminded him that we wanted him to insert an aircraft, which he did. It's a DC-3 (C-47). Sloane's paintings are unique in that he paints on wood rather than canvas.

Some weeks later he called and we made a date to pick up the painting and offered to take him to dinner. We ate at a local restaurant of his choice. He told us that he had taken up flying in order to see the clouds up close and be better able to paint them. In our opinion he is an artist who beautifully depicts the amazing vast panorama of sky and clouds as a pilot experiences them! During the meal he was drawing on the tablecloth. When I asked him about it he said it was of my hand. It turned out he was sketching my hand throughout dinner. I should have kept the tablecloth. I did keep two small aperitif glasses that I admired and Eric gave me.

When we picked up the painting, he had framed it in a lovely antiqued, gray wormwood frame.

**We proudly display this painting in our home to this day!**

We had occasion to meet Eric Sloane once again in March 1973. He was exhibiting at the Poinciana Gallery in Palm Beach, Florida, and was selling his book *I Remember America*. He remembered us and offered to buy back his painting. Of course we didn't want to sell but were curious as to why he would purchase his own painting. His reply was that he would burn it, making the rest of his collection that much more valuable.

We purchased his book and on the inside cover he quickly drew a Stearman flying over a covered bridge with the inscription "To the Haydu Library–Eric Sloane."

## More Airplanes

In May 1971 we purchased another prize winning PT-17 Stearman N9298H which had been restored by Al Li Calzi, Bridgeton, New Jersey. We had the pleasure of exhibiting this Stearman at many air shows.

After having fun with this plane, we went back to a more practical one that would accommodate our family for cross-country flying. We were also looking for the safety feature of two engines. In May 1974 we purchased a twin-engine Beechcraft D-55 Baron N533Q. It was always great to visit our children who by then were in college. Joey attended Bryant College; Steve, Johnson & Wales, both in Rhode Island. Diana chose the University of South Florida, Tampa. During the winter when we vacationed in Florida, we would fly our plane to visit her or bring her to the east coast of Florida, where we had a condominium.

Frequently we would fly friends to Treasure Cay, the Bahamas, to play golf. It was close enough (about 60 miles over water) that we could fly there, play eighteen holes of golf and be back in Florida for dinner.

## And Still More Airplanes

After the twin Beech came the T-34A, Beech A-45 N5MT, another single engine, two place aircraft that had been manufactured in August 1955 and later restored. In 1975 after selling the T-34 we were back in a four-seater airplane known as Cessna 210 N5234V, which we sold in 1976. This was followed by a Beech Debonaire, F-33A N77KG, a single engine, four place aircraft, which we flew to lots of places and kept until 1983.

In 1984 guess what we bought next? Yes, another Stearman Nl242V. This had been restored by someone at North Perry Airport, Florida, and was also another beautiful restoration. It was always fun to take this type of aircraft to air shows where so many who had flown them in World War II would come by to reminisce. We sold the Stearman and then owned several Cessna 172s. Our son, Steve was now flying, and he bought one of the Cessnas.

## Hangar Party

At one time we had two airplanes, a Cessna 172 and the Stearman. We kept them in our hangar at Lantana Airport, Lantana, Florida. Many of our friends and their families were in Florida and had heard us talk so much about flying that we thought they might enjoy a ride. We decided it would be fun to give a Hangar Party. We settled on a date, invited a group of friends and arranged for refreshments (no alcoholic beverages). I flew the women in the Cessna and Joe flew the men in the Stearman. One of the men was so enthralled he started taking flying lessons.

**It was a unique party on a perfect day and a wonderful time was had by all!**

## Real Estate Ventures

In 1958 Joe and I purchased a 220 acre farm in Fredon, Sussex County, New Jersey, thinking it would be an ideal place to live. However, after realizing the amount of time it would take for him to commute to Newark, where his meat business was located, we decided it was not practical at that time. We felt it would be better to allow the children to finish high school in Livingston, where they had grown up. It was the purchase of this farm that spurred our interest in real estate.

Joe experienced some serious health problems and in 1967 sold his interests in S. Haydu & Sons to his three remaining brothers.

In 1969 Joe and I studied for and earned our real estate licenses and became affiliated with Martin, Holenstein and Zamos, Newton, Sussex County, New Jersey, on a part time basis. In addition to the listings in the office, we traveled throughout Sussex and Warren Counties searching for farms to purchase that had considerable road frontage. We would subdivide from the existing road frontage into smaller parcels, which we were able to do by applying for minor subdivisions. This kept the costs lower than if we had applied for major subdivisions. We continued doing this with about ten different farms over the years.

In 1972, after all the children graduated from Livingston High School, we sold our house at 22 Chestnut Street, and moved to a home in Frelinghuysen Township, Warren County to be closer to our real estate activities. Eventually we sold that and moved to Florida on a permanent basis. We could still remain active in our real estate ventures from there. By then the children were following their own careers.

# TWELVE

# RACES AND CONTESTS

### First Air Race

In May 1965 I entered my first airplane race. It was from Caldwell-Wright Airport, Fairfield, New Jersey, to Nassau in the Bahamas in the Cessna 172 N9831T lent to me by our friend Calvin Theobold. Although you could have a copilot, I decided to fly solo (I didn't want anyone to see any mistakes I might make). It is not a race as in a horse or car race where the first one in is the winner. There are many varieties of aircraft that enter, some faster than others. To be fair to all aircraft, allowing the slower planes to compete against the faster ones, a formula is established giving each one a handicap.

The name given this annual race is Angel Derby. You have to fly a certain route with mandatory landings at designated airports. Our route was Caldwell, New Jersey; Dulles Airport, Washington, D.C.; Greensboro, North Carolina; Macon, Georgia; Daytona, Florida; Fort Lauderdale, Florida; Nassau, Bahamas. From Fort Lauderdale to Nassau we had to fly over a large stretch of the Atlantic Ocean. I was concerned about flying over so much water in a single engine aircraft, so I flew quite high not taking advantage

*Bee immediately after landing in Nassau.*

of stronger tail winds at lower altitudes. This cost me time and I came in second in my class. Of the thirty-eight who entered the race, thirty-five finished. On the return trip, I was upset with my self for being 'chicken', so when leaving Nassau, I flew very low. The water was so clear I could see sharks stalking their prey. It was an awesome sight!

*In the June 5, 1965, "National Provisioner," magazine the following was printed:*
   *"SURVIVAL KIT is presented by Joseph Haydu, President of S. Haydu & Sons, Newark, N. J., to his wife, Bernice, at start of her solo flight in recent New Jersey-to-Nassau speed race for women. The kit contained her favorite Haydu meat products. Both Haydu's are accomplished fliers, each with more than twenty years and 2,000 hours of experience. Mrs. Haydu flew in a single-engine plane in the 1,300-mile race over land and water."*

## Bahama Treasure Hunt

The Ministry of Tourism in Nassau, Bahamas, was anxious to promote flying there by private aircraft. Each fall they ran a contest called the Treasure Hunt.

In the fall of 1966 Joe and I entered this challenging and entertaining event. It started at a party in Nassau where we were given a list of clues. These clues were pictures of an object (such as a light house) 'somewhere' on one of the many islands of the Bahamas. The area to be covered was extensive. You were supposed to fly around, identify the pictured clue and note its latitude and longitude. The person or couple who logged the most clues was the winner. The first prize was a building lot on one of the islands, at that time worth $6000. Among the many contestants there were four shrewd couples. They divided the area into quadrants allowing each couple to thoroughly search its quad for clues. They pooled their findings and, of course, won the Treasure Hunt! Nonetheless, the event was lots of fun with many hosted parties and numerous smaller prizes.

# Powder Puff Derby Race

The Powder Puff Derbies were the really long races–2,000 or 3,000 miles–usually from one coast to the other.

In 1929 Bobbi Trout, Amelia Earhart, Florence Pancho Barnes and seventeen other participants established the first All Women's Transcontinental Air Race from Santa Monica, California, to Cleveland, Ohio. Humorist Will Rogers dubbed it the Powder Puff Derby and the name stuck.

In July 1967 I entered the 21st annual Powder Puff Race, again solo. It started in Atlantic City, New Jersey, and terminated in Torrance, California, some 3000 miles. There are cash prizes for these races, although they never come near the expense of entering and flying. Women fly the races for the challenge. In this race there was a $3000 purse to be divided among the first five places.

Graham Denham of Aero Service Co., Millville Airport, New Jersey, offered me the use of his Cherokee 140 N6918W. He painted the name "Miss Millville" on the side of the plane. Not to be outdone, husband Joe hung a banner on the plane reading "California Here We Come. Good Luck–Haydu Meats." The races are only flown VFR (visual flight rules). The start was delayed for two days because of bad weather. Actually, it should not have started even then. There were aircraft that had the fuel capacity to by-pass the first airport check point which was <u>not</u> a mandatory landing one. Unfortunately, mine was not one of them and I had to stop there for fuel–Martinsburg, West Virginia.

Later, in response to a request from the public relations consultants handling this race, I reported as follows:

"About thirty of the ships had enough fuel capacity to by-pass the first gas stop. Lucky them–the weather permitted them to get into and out of Cincinnati, Ohio, before the weather closed in. The rest of the aircraft (seventy took off from Atlantic City) had to go to Martinsburg for fuel. There we received weather reports showing Cincinnati to be instrument or marginal weather. I waited for three, hourly weather sequences, which revealed that conditions in Cincinnati were improving. It was stated that if we did not get out of Martinsburg on Monday, we would be weathered in the next day. Thirteen of us decided to leave, hoping the weather would hold until our arrival in Cincinnati.

Going over the Blue Ridge Mountains at very low altitudes, which I won't state on the grounds the figures might incriminate me, I had to deviate from course and go around thunderstorms. I was still OK unti about forty-five miles west of Parkersburg, West Virginia. Here I was flying about 200' above the rolling West Virginia hills when I ran into clouds. Since I did not want to become another 'statistic', I made a 180 degree turn to Parkersburg, West Virginia. I found company there because five other aircraft that had left Martinsburg at the same time were also there. A few minutes after we landed, the airport was closed to visual flight rules."

There were seven other aircraft caught in the same predicament scattered in the area at various other airports. The rules of the race read, 'that if you are over-night at other than a designated airport you are eliminated.' When I called back to headquarters, I found that for the first leg of the race I had been among the top ten. Had I finished anywhere in the top ten, I would have considered this a major victory for a first Powder Puff Race.

In Parkersburg a great fuss was made about all of us. We were interviewed for a front-page story in the *Parkersburg Press* and the Chamber of Commerce treated us to dinner.

One of the other contestants, Laura Zerener, wrote me about her harrowing experience on this trip:

"As you know, we didn't plan to stop at Martinsburg and continued on to Cincinnatti. After being clocked at Baltimore, we began a slow climb and were making fairly good time. Around Parkersburg, encountered thickly scattered clouds and began to descend to try to get under the weather. Ended our descent at 1500 – 2000 feet in a solid overcast which we couldn't under-fly. Couldn't pick up any VOR (very high frequency omni range) at that altitude either. Well, I was scared silly so throttled back on the power, but held my course and flew on instruments (No, no plan)*, kept our navigation channel volume up trying to pick up some directional assistance but didn't have any luck. Finally, with our fuel running very low, I turned up the volume on the communications and heard Cincinnati calling us. Replied, asking them for radar. They bounded right back saying we were too low to be picked up, but told me to key my mike for a DF** steer. Just as I released the key, we broke out of the weather (after about an hour in it) and were right over the Ohio River.

When we landed and refueled, we found that we had ten gallons left–six usable–which would have kept us up about fifteen more minutes! Speaking of statistics, I had been sure that we were at least two! We put our arms around each other and said 'We won.' I wanted to quit, at least for the day but the FAA told us that if we didn't go on, we would be weathered in there for at least two days. All we had on the leg to Springfield was a solid line of thunderstorms, which we had to detour around. Am sorry you didn't get to finish – and we missed seeing more of you."

*In order to fly under instrument conditions, you must file an instrument flight plan with the flight service either on the ground by telephone or while airborne.

**Directional Flight instrument assists those on the ground following your flight via radar.

*Bee on the wing of the Piper Cherokee she flew in the 21st Powder Puff Derby*

## Another Powder Puff Derby

At the beginning of 1971 I was approached by Eleanor "Ellie" Schapira who wanted to fly in the 25th Powder Puff Derby and asked me if I would be the pilot. She had a private pilot's license but wanted to fly with someone who had more flying experience. David Loeser of Somerset, New Jersey, lent us his Comanche 260 N8639P. We would pay all expenses and damages (if any) that might accrue during the race.

The race dates were July 5-8, 1971, and it started in Calgary, Canada, terminating in Baton Rouge, Louisiana. This was the first time the Transcontinental Air Race started outside the United States.

We started from Morristown Airport, New Jersey, for Calgary on June 26th  The weather to the west was bad so we elected to fly north and then west. We got as far as Muskegon, Michigan.  On June 27th we stopped at Rapid City, South Dakota, but not before flying as close to Mt. Rushmore as possible to take pictures of the likenesses of George Washington, Thomas Jefferson, Theodore Roosevelt and Abraham Lincoln carved from granite rock six thousand feet high on the mountain. June 28th we made it to Cody, Wyoming, hired a car and drove 240 miles to Yellowstone National Park.

June 29th we arrived in Calgary and since we had three days before any required activities prior to the race, we hired a car and drove to Lake Louise, Banff, Canada.  En route to Lake Louise we saw many brown bears, a moose and other wild life. The mountains in that area are spectacular.

Even though this was July the weather at the lake was extremely cold. We had to borrow winter ski jackets when venturing onto the Columbia Ice Field Glacier.

The race started on July 5th. There were 150 entrants and we were assigned number 100. It was late in the day before we started. The first leg did not go well. We encountered heavy head winds and experienced trouble in receiving signals from the radio frequencies, no doubt because of the mountainous terrain. These problems on the first leg of the flight caused us to lose time, which resulted in our finishing in the last quarter.

The race itself is tiring because you have to get up very early to be off at daybreak but must be on the ground at official nightfall. With so many entrants it was often difficult to get early transportation to the airport from where we were staying overnight. Our route was Great Falls and Billings, Montana; Rapid City, South Dakota; Denver, Colorado; McCook and Lincoln, Nebraska; St. Louis, Missouri; Little Rock, Arkansas; and Baton Rouge, Louisiana.

We were thrilled to see Joe, Diana and my friend Betty Kergan who had driven to Baton Rouge to greet us and enjoy the final festivities. They loved us even though we didn't win.

*Bee and Ellie Schapira planning for 25th Powder Puff Derby.*

*Joe, Bee, Betty and Diana prior to the banquet at the terminus of the race.*

# THIRTEEN

# THE LUCKIEST DAY OF MY LIFE

In August 1971 we had been invited to an air show in Ottawa, Canada, to display our restored, award winning, PT-17 Stearman. At the beginning of the show the restored aircraft there for display are asked to do a 'fly-by' which means you fly over a runway at low altitude to display your airplane. We were having a problem with our brakes and were not able to participate. Ken Henderson a friend we had known from attending other air shows, invited me to fly with him while doing the fly-by. He owned a PT-26 World War II plane he had just finished restoring.

In a letter I wrote to a friend later, I described what happened:

"Ken Henderson is an airline pilot with 22,000 hours and had been trained in World War II. He invited me to fly in his airplane while he did his fly-by. I guess Ken must have gotten 'crowd fever' or something because during the second fly-by, he pulled up, dissipating speed and then without any warning started into a roll. This was within 300' to 400' above the ground.

The moment he started this maneuver I knew we would never recover. We were going too slow, he had the nose of the aircraft too high and we were too low to be able to recover. At about 100' above the ground I looked down being able to look over his head (I was in the back)–that is how steep an angle we were in–I saw that we were headed for telephone poles and a road. We were still in a partial bank* with the left wing down. I did not see how we were going to get out of this alive. I thought, You're going to die. I was sad because I did not want to die but I was resigned–no hysterics.

I blacked out, felt a lot of jostling around and when my vision came back we were stopped in a newly plowed field. I quickly undid my seat-belt and opened the hatch**. Ken was doing the same. We both ran from the plane fearing it might explode into flames. It did not. We found out later, the gas tanks were not ruptured. As we ran from the plane, I realized I was hurt. By this time a crowd was assembling. I must have been bleeding profusely, because someone took off his shirt and wrapped it around my head.

Soon an ambulance and doctor arrived to take us to the Ottawa Civic Hospital. My upper left arm was broken in two places. The hatch had slammed closed on my right hand, I must have put my hand there to brace myself. I had a large cut on my forehead. It took twenty-five stitches. Fortunately, it was just in the hairline. I was bruised and cut all over. It seems we hit at nine Gs*** and the aircraft tubing (frame) near my cockpit bent. We hit so hard that the back of the seat was released from its position allowing my body to be thrown forward. Miraculously, the shoulder straps held. Ken's seat broke and he had two cuts on his forehead. They were able to release him from the hospital the same day.

I spent a week in the hospital in Ottawa. Joey and Stevey flew to Canada so that Joey could accompany me home by airline and Stevey was his Dad's copilot on the way home in the Stearman. My left arm is unusable

*The remains of PT-26 aircraft after crash August 16, 1971.*

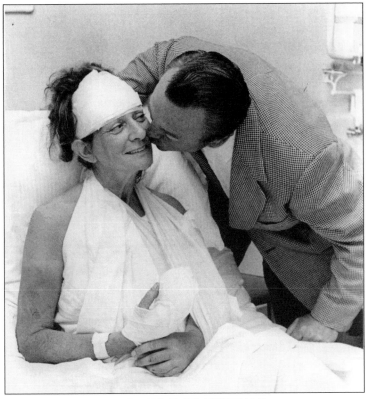

**SHE LIVED TO TELL THE TALE.**
*Bernice Haydu gets a comforting kiss today from hubby, Joe.*

but will mend in time–they say six months. Three fingers of my right hand cannot function yet, but I am told in time and with therapy they should be OK. The tip is off the finger next to my index finger.

I learned later how we hit. First we hit in a cornfield just before the telephone poles. Either at that time, or just before, Ken too blacked out and it was out of our hands. This first hit jumped us up in the air enough to miss a ditch but the left wing hit the first telephone pole shearing the wing off just at the gas tank. This diverted the path of the airplane from a head-on collision into the telephone pole across the street. After hitting the first pole, we skidded across the street and the right wing hit the next telephone pole so hard that it cracked the pole. Again, the wing was severed at the tank. We bounced along the newly plowed field and stopped. Needless to say, there was nothing left of the prop and the airplane was declared a 'total'****.

The recuperation is no walk in the park. They were able to set my left arm without any incisions. I have to keep it in a down position. My right hand, however, has to be kept in an upright position. That means I cannot lie down to sleep and have to accustom my self to sleep sitting up.

I need to exercise my right hand with a small rubber ball. My forehead remains numb. In my present condition I can't do much. I am helped with everything by my wonderful family–even to typing.

I guess you know what my real name is–LUCKY! To this day I marvel that I came out of that airplane alive. I must say this, Ken's foolish judgment got us into this predicament but his experience and perseverance in trying to right us saved our lives. Had we hit at an angle, or nose down, I am sure we would have been killed."

* Bank means to turn.

** Hatch is a cover over the cockpit which slides open or closed as desired.

*** G is a unit of acceleration equal to thirty-two feet per second, per second.

**** Total means the plane was so badly damaged it could not be rebuilt.

The Ottawa Citizen newspaper of August 15, 1971, featured an article under the heading

## "DEATH WAITED, AND MISSED"

# **BATTLE FOR RECOGNITION**

Often in researching the WASP history you will read a brief sentence stating the WASP received recognition as veterans of World War II in 1977. Well, it didn't 'just happen'. There is more to the story and hopefully this will give you some insight into the events that made it possible.

In 1972 the WASP convened for a Thirtieth Anniversary Reunion in Sweetwater, Texas. Colonel Bruce Arnold, son of General "Hap" Arnold, had been invited as guest speaker. It was then he promised to see what he could do to help us attain status as veterans of World War II. After working with Bruce, I realized he took on this monumental task for two reasons. One was his desire to fulfill the wishes of his father who had been the head of the Army Air Force during the war but who had died in 1950. The other was that he had a sincere appreciation of the WASP contributions to their country. He admired them, and wanted to see them treated fairly.

At the 1975 Reno, Nevada, WASP reunion, I was elected president of our organization, Order of Fifinella. Fifinella is the good luck lady gremlin designed by Walt Disney to fly with the WASP in World War II. After we were disbanded we adopted her name for our organization.

It was during my two terms as president 1975–1978 that we made our concerted effort to gain recognition as veterans from Congress. Leading us every step of the way was Colonel Bruce Arnold.

Knowing the need to provide Congress with the technical information they would require, Bruce set up a Militarization Committee. He divided it into three parts, assigning each part to a different WASP.

(1) Dora Dougherty Strother–to list the accomplishments of the WASP.

(2) Byrd Granger–to prove we had been treated as military.

(3) Doris Tanner-to compare our training and monetary compensation with that of cadets and officers.

We learned that in March 1975, Bill S.R. 1345 to recognize WASP as veterans had been introduced to the Senate Veterans Affairs Committee by Senator Barry Goldwater. Senator Goldwater had been a pilot with the Air Transport Command during the war and had flown with the women out of New Castle, Delaware.

Senator Vance Hartke, Indiana, Chairman of the Veterans Affairs Committee would not allow the bill out of committee nor would he allow a hearing.

In May 1975 House Representatives Burleson and Patsy T. Mink introduced an identical bill, Bill H.R. 6595 to the House Veterans Affairs Committee with the same result.

September 10, 1976, Bill S.R. 71 was introduced by Vance Hartke to give Polish and Czechoslovakian forces who served under British and French Command during World Wars I and II as allies of the United States and who have been United States citizens for ten years, hospital and medical care– the same as offered to our veterans. Now one might wonder why Hartke would suppress the 1,074 WASP who were citizens at the time they served, in favor of these approximately 40,000 Polish and Czechoslovakians who were not citizens at the time they were fighting. We learned Hartke was running for reelection that year and had a large Polish and Czechoslovakian constituency in Indiana.

Senator Goldwater requested an amendment to this bill to include the WASP. In his remarks on the Senate floor, he said:

"Although they were hired as civilians, they did not enjoy freedom as civilians. As far as the Air Force was concerned, they were in the Air Force. They were paid military scale salaries, slightly less than a second lieutenant, they lived at Air Force bases, they ate in mess halls, they were under military discipline and subject to all military rules and regulations. However, they received no veteran's benefits, nor government insurance. Thirty-eight of them gave their lives in performance of military flight duty for their country. In my opinion, it is outrageous to deny the surviving women who rendered this service–and who probably do not number over 900–entitlement to at least medical and hospital benefits. The recognition of their service is the important thing, not the small amount of benefits that a few women would receive under the amendment. This group of women was shunted aside by the country they served; and it is better that we should correct a past wrong now, rather than leave the record blemished."

Bill S.R. 71 with Senator Goldwater's amendment passed the Senate by a voice vote.

September 14, 1976, this same bill came before the House of Representatives Veterans Affairs Committee. It had passed on July 21,

*Our Board of Directors: Seated, Sara Hayden, Vice President; Leota Deaton; Bee Haydu, President. Standing; Betty Nicholas, Secretary/Treasurer; Betty Cross, Newsletter Editor; Marty Wyall.*

1975, without Senator Goldwater's amendment and was re-introduced for another vote including this amendment. The House did not want to pass this bill with Goldwater's amendment. The chairman of the Veterans Affairs Committee for the House, Ray Roberts, stated on the floor on September 14, 1976, that the amendment proposed by Senator Goldwater "is strongly opposed by the American Legion, the Disabled American Veterans and the Veterans of Foreign Wars."

During that session, the only thing that Senator Goldwater was able to do in both House and Senate Veterans Affairs Committees was extract a promise in writing that in 1977 the WASP would be granted hearings.

### Our work was laid out for us.

In addition to running the normal activities of the organization, the board was called upon to do many other things. We had to solicit funds for what we realized would be a long battle in Washington, D.C. The treasury contained a meager amount when we took office and was not sufficient to carry on a protracted fight on a national level, much less pay the expenses of running the organization.

We had to locate 'lost' WASP.

The membership had to be motivated to lobby their Washington representatives and to seek publicity in their home states.
AND

We had to keep abreast of what was needed and always mindful of our funds, or rather lack of, we would try to meet, eat and stay overnight at one of our member's homes. We also paid our own way to meetings, conventions, etc.

### This was becoming a full time job!

*There were many meetings such as this one March 17, 1977, in Senator Barry Goldwater's office, Washington, D.C. Here the Militarization Committee prepare for the upcoming hearing before the Senate Veterans Affairs Committee. Pictured with Senator Goldwater are Lee Wheelwright, Dr. Dora Strother,* Bernice Falk Haydu,* Dr. Byrd Granger, Margaret Boylan,* Doris Tanner,* Colonel Bruce, Arnold.* *
*\* Testified at the May 25, 1977, Senate Hearings as did Senator Goldwater.*

It was at this meeting that we presented Senator Goldwater with a pair of 14k gold WASP wings and the following Citation.

*May 25, 1977, outside the Senate Hearing Room where the Veterans Affairs Committee chaired by Senator Alan Cranston heard testimony. Many WASP came from around the country to attend this hearing.*

Many other than WASP volunteered to help. Some had been flight instructors in Sweetwater. Months were spent locating our lost WASP. Those who responded donated their time, spoke before organizations explaining our predicament, got signatures on petitions, contacted congressional representatives and any other VIPs we could think of and above all generated as much positive publicity as possible locally and nationally. We urged the WASP to visit Washington and talk to their representatives educating them concerning what we had done.

Thanks to Colonel Arnold, we had a small headquarters office in the Army Navy Club in D.C. Here we assembled newspaper and magazine articles in large albums, divided by state. When a WASP visited D. C. we would lend her the album to show her representatives how much publicity was generated in her particular state and how important it was to her representatives' constituents. This was a very significant strategy and favorably impressed our legislators.

We had to get the news to our scattered members quickly since things would change almost daily. We had a Wasp Newsletter under the capable editorship of Betty Cross. I would send her articles and updates on D.C. activities but by the time the newsletter was printed and circulated, it was often old news. We were fortunate to have the publishers of a weekly newspaper, The Stars and Stripes–The National Tribune, offer to devote a column to our activities. They hired WASP Patricia Collins Hughes to write this column and we urged our members to subscribe to the newspaper so they could obtain current information.

Thinking it would be a good idea to show that a great number of people were concerned about our status, I penned the following petition which was distributed to WASP all over the country for them to gather signatures:

"We the undersigned respectfully request the passage of the Senate Bill S.R. 247 and the House of Representatives Bill 3321 to grant the WASP (Women Airforce Service Pilots) of World War II military status. This status was denied them in 1944.

These heroic women served in a military capacity, wore uniforms, were subject to military discipline and courtesy. They flew every military airplane manufactured for World War II and served their country replacing men pilots for active duty overseas.

They also risked their lives daily and 38 of these women died in the service of their country.

The WASP who lived on Army Air Force bases were paid less than flying Air Force Officers and were not allowed military funerals or insurance or any other benefits given men who served.

Needed now, not posthumously, is militarization that would give them the recognition and the rights they so justly deserve. The 850 remaining who are in need of veterans' benefits should be given them through the militarization process.

We feel this country does not often have the opportunity to right the wrongs done in the past, but this is one time we can."

**We succeeded in gathering over 22,000 signatures!**

*September 20, 1977, On the steps of the Capitol where the House of Representatives Veterans Affairs Committee, chaired by the Honorable Ray Roberts, heard testimony. Bernice Haydu presented Congressman James Quillen, Congresswomen Margaret Heckler and Lindy Boggs signatures of over 22,000 people from all over the United States favoring recognition for the WASP.*

During the September 20th Hearing the chairman of the Veterans Affairs Committee, the Honorable Ray Roberts, left the meeting for a moment. I followed him into the hall. I recall that he shook his finger at me as he said in his good-old-boy Texas drawl off-the-record, "I promised you girls a hearing. Well, you're getting it. But I promise you this, young lady, the bill will never leave my committee."

**That is what we were up against!**

It was the wonderful women in government who finally helped us push this through. Congresswomen Lindy Boggs and Margaret Heckler introduced identically worded bills and convinced every woman member of Congress to do the same–a FIRST. Some testified at the Hearings. Assistant Secretary of the Air Force Antonia Handler Chayes was an expert witness for the WASP. She had convinced the Department of Defense to back us. It became the only piece of legislation in history to be cosponsored by EVERY woman member of Congress. One of the long overdue items included in the WASP bill was for the women telephone operators of World War I to be recognized as war veterans. They had never been given this status in spite of the fact they were stationed in the front line trenches side by side with the fighting soldiers.

All the WASP who could, arrived in Washington in their Santiago blue uniforms to show their solidarity. Letters, telegrams and telephone calls descended on Congress.

In the meantime Arnold was preparing a last ditch defense. He sent a packet with copies of documents we had, proving we were supposed to have become a part of the Air Force, to each member of the House Veterans Affairs Committee just prior to our Hearing. One of these documents was an honorable discharge stating that she had "Honorably served in the Army of the United States." Congressman Olin "Tiger" Teague, a member of this committee and one of our strongest opponents, was surprised when he saw this discharge and was heard to say, "It reads just like mine." It seems this small piece of paper might have been a deciding factor tipping the scales in favor of the WASP.

### Once again Bruce Arnold had come to our rescue!

On November 3, 1977, the House passed the bill.
On November 4th the Senate passed it.
On November 23, 1977, President James Carter signed:

### PUBLIC LAW #95-202, SECTION 401 THE G.I. BILL IMPROVEMENT ACT OF 1977

### SOME NEWS ARTICLES AND HEADLINES

*One of the pictures included in the 1976 syndicated news article by David Langford. Joe and Bee Haydu at the Neptune plant going over a planned trip while Joey and Steve look on.*

*Bee at Asbury Park Airport, New Jersey, putting into action a planned trip to be taken in an open cockpit aircraft.*

153

# Appearances and Publicity Were Prolific

At the P-47 Thunderbolt Pilots Association reunion in New York City, Bee was presented with a plaque for her efforts on behalf of the WASP. The inscription reads: "Presented to Mrs. Bee Haydu, President WASP, Women Airforce Service Pilots WWII 16th Annual P-47 Thunderbolt Pilots Reunion May 7, 1977". Bee obtained many signatures on the petition at this reunion.

May 11, 1977, TV Show "Good Morning America" David Hartman and Sandy Hill interviewed Bernice "Bee" Haydu, Velta Benn and Senator Barry Goldwater (who was being televised from Washington, D.C.)

May 24, 1977, TV Interview in Washington, D. C. on a program called "Panorama"— Moderator, Bee Haydu, F. Lee Bailey,* Lorraine Rodgers, Paul Garber from Smithsonian Air and Space Museum, the same person to whom I had given my uniform in 1969.

* Not there to speak about the WASP.

*November 9, 1977, TV show–"To Tell the Truth"–Clare Goode, Bernice Bee Haydu, Fran Slotkin. Clare and Fran were the "impostors." They knew little or nothing about the WASP. I had to take an oath that I would tell the truth–they did not. We met the day before and in about two hours I gave them enough information to enable them to give authentic sounding answers. Theirs was the most difficult task.*

*To Tell The Truth panel, Bill McCullough, Kitty Carlile, Orson Beane, Peggy Cass. Only one of the panel guessed Bee as the real Bee Haydu. This proves what a good job the 'impostors' did.*

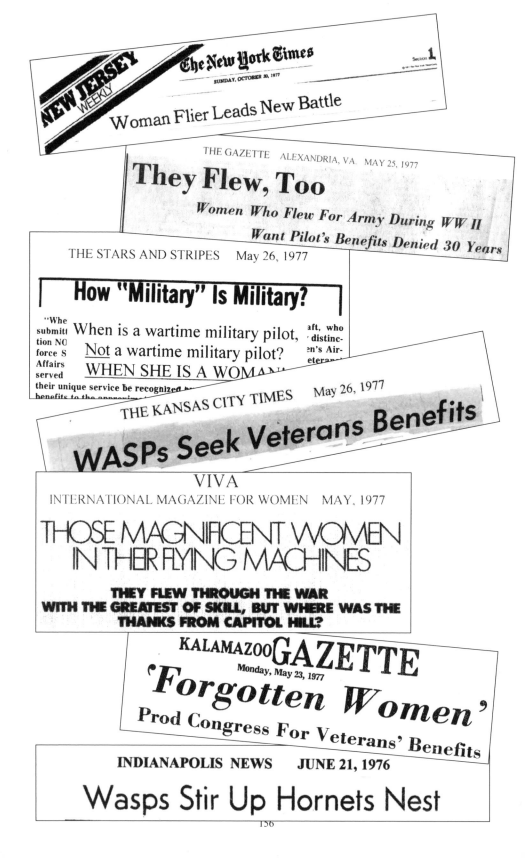

**NEW JERSEY** WEEKLY

### The New York Times

SUNDAY, OCTOBER 30, 1977

Section **1**

## Woman Flier Leads New Battle

---

THE GAZETTE   ALEXANDRIA, VA.   MAY 25, 1977

# They Flew, Too

### Women Who Flew For Army During WW II
### Want Pilot's Benefits Denied 30 Years

---

THE STARS AND STRIPES    May 26, 1977

## How "Military" Is Military?

When is a wartime military pilot,
Not a wartime military pilot?
WHEN SHE IS A WOMAN

their unique service be recognized

---

THE KANSAS CITY TIMES    May 26, 1977

## WASPs Seek Veterans Benefits

---

## VIVA

INTERNATIONAL MAGAZINE FOR WOMEN    MAY, 1977

# THOSE MAGNIFICENT WOMEN IN THEIR FLYING MACHINES

### THEY FLEW THROUGH THE WAR WITH THE GREATEST OF SKILL, BUT WHERE WAS THE THANKS FROM CAPITOL HILL?

---

KALAMAZOO **GAZETTE**

Monday, May 23, 1977

# 'Forgotten Women'
### Prod Congress For Veterans' Benefits

---

INDIANAPOLIS NEWS    JUNE 21, 1976

# Wasps Stir Up Hornets Nest

"THEY ARE the forgotten heroines of World War II, some 1000 spunky young women who flew warplanes on thankless but dangerous missions at home so the men could go to battle on the enemy's turf.

In their baggy GI-issue overalls which they dubbed their 'zoot suits' and struggling with 30-pound parachutes, they logged 60 million miles, ferrying fighters and bombers to points of embarkation, towing targets for combat pilots and anti-aircraft batteries to shoot at, flight-testing new aircraft or training other pilots in instrument navigation.

When one was killed, as thirty-eight of them were, they sometimes had to pass the hat for money to send the body home for burial. They called themselves the 'guinea pigs'. They were housed in barracks, marched to meals, did calisthenics and were hauled to classes in Army trucks with wooden seats they called 'cattle cars'.

The WASP would go on to fly the hot pursuit planes such as the P-51, P-40, P-47, P-38 and P-39 on domestic missions, or the twin-engine bombers–B-25 and B-26. Two WASP were checked out in the Super-fortress B-29. Another flew the jet fighter, which was just coming onto the scene.

Mrs. Bernice Haydu who helps her husband run a hot dog packing business in Neptune City, New Jersey said 'Nothing makes a WASP madder than for the Air Force to intimate that its new undergraduate pilot training program for females is a first. The WASP were the first. When you talk about a WASP today, people think you are talking about White Anglo-Saxon Protestant.'

Cornelia Fort, 24, of Nashville, Tennessee, was the first of the thirty-eight women to die while flying for American military forces. An eyewitness to the Japanese invasion of Pearl Harbor from the cockpit of a tiny Piper Cub, she later joined the Women's Auxiliary Ferrying Squadron, a forerunner to the WASP program.

Before she was killed in a bomber crash in Texas, Fort wrote in the *Woman's Home Companion* magazine about the experiences of the female pilots. This is the article written by Cornelia for the July 1942 issue. Her words will live as a moving account of why one woman joined the WAFS and as a testament to all American women who are helping keep America free."

# Cornelia Fort's Magazine Article

"I knew I was going to join the Women's Auxiliary Ferrying Squadron before the organization was a reality, before it had a name, before it was anything but a radical idea in the minds of a few men who believed that women could fly airplanes. But I never knew it so surely as I did in Honolulu on December 7, 1941. At dawn that morning I drove from Waikiki to the John Rodgers civilian airport right next to Pearl Harbor, where I was a civilian pilot instructor. Shortly after six-thirty I began landing and takeoff practice with my regular student. Coming in just before the last landing, I looked casually around and saw a military plane coming directly toward me. I jerked the controls away from my student and jammed the throttle wide open to pull above the oncoming plane. He passed so close under us that our celluloid windows rattled violently and I looked down to see what kind of plane it was.

The painted red balls on the tops of the wings shone brightly in the sun. I looked again with complete and utter disbelief. Honolulu was familiar with the emblem of the Rising Sun on passenger ships but not on airplanes.

I looked quickly at Pearl Harbor and my spine tingled when I saw billowing black smoke. Still I thought hollowly it might be some kind of coincidence or maneuvers, it might be, it must be. For surely, dear God…

Then I looked way up and saw the formations of silver bombers riding in. Something detached itself from an airplane and came glistening down. My eyes followed it down, down and even with knowledge pounding in my mind, my heart turned convulsively when the bomb exploded in the middle of the harbor. I knew the air was not the place for my little baby airplane and I set about landing as quickly as ever I could. A few seconds later a shadow passed over me and simultaneously bullets spattered all around me.

Suddenly that little wedge of sky above Hickam Field and Pearl Harbor was the busiest fullest piece of sky I ever saw.

We counted anxiously as our little civilian planes came flying home to roost. Two never came back. They were washed ashore weeks later on the windward side of the island, bullet-riddled. Not a pretty way for the brave little yellow cubs and their pilots to go down to death.

The rest of December 7th has been described by too many in too much detail for me to reiterate. I remained on the island until three months later when I returned by convoy to the United States. None of the pilots wanted to leave but there was no civilian flying in the islands after the attack. And each of us had some individual score to settle with the Japs who had brought murder and destruction to our islands.

When I returned, the only way I could fly at all was to instruct Civilian Pilot Training programs. Weeks passed. Then, out of the blue, came a telegram from the War Department announcing the organization of the WAFS and the order to report within twenty-four hours if interested. I left at once.

Mrs. Nancy Love was appointed Senior Squadron Leader of the WAFS by the secretary of war. No better choice could have been made. First and most important she is a good pilot, has tremendous enthusiasm and belief in women pilots and did a wonderful job in helping us to be accepted on an equal status with men.

Because there were and are so many disbelievers in women pilots, especially in their place in the army, officials wanted the best possible qualifications to go with the first experimental group. All of us realized what a spot we were on. We had to deliver the goods or else. Or else there wouldn't ever be another chance for women pilots in any part of the service.

We have no hopes of replacing men pilots. But we can each release a man to combat, to faster ships, to overseas work. Delivering a trainer to Texas may be as important as delivering a bomber to Africa if you take the long view. We are beginning to prove that women can be trusted to deliver airplanes safely and in the doing serve the country, which is our country too.

I have yet to have a feeling, which approaches in satisfaction that of having signed, sealed and delivered an airplane for the United States Army. The attitude that most non-flyers have about pilots is distressing and often acutely embarrassing. They chatter about the glamour of flying. Well, any pilot can tell you how glamorous it is. We get up in the cold dark in order to get to the airport by daylight. We wear heavy cumbersome flying clothes and a thirty-pound parachute. You are either cold or hot. If you are female your lipstick wears off and your hair gets straighter and straighter. You look forward all afternoon to the bath you will have and the steak. Well, we get the bath but seldom the steak. Sometimes we are too tired to eat and fall wearily into bed.

None of us can put into words why we fly. It is something different for each of us. I can't say exactly why I fly but I know why as I've never known anything in my life. I knew it when I saw my plane silhouetted against the clouds framed by a circular rainbow.* I knew it when I flew up into the extinct volcano Haleakala on the island of Maui and saw the gray-green pineapple fields slope down to the cloud-dappled blueness of the Pacific. But I know it otherwise than in beauty. I know it in dignity and self-sufficiency and in the pride of skill. I know it in the satisfaction of usefulness.

For all the girls in the WAFS, I think the most concrete moment of happiness came at our first review. Suddenly and for the first time we felt a part of something larger. Because of our uniforms, which we had earned, we were marching with the men, marching with all the freedom loving people in the world.

And then, while we were standing at attention, a bomber took off followed by four fighters. We knew the bomber was headed across the ocean and that the fighters were going to escort it part way. As they circled over us I could hardly see them for the tears in my eyes. It was striking symbolism and I think all of us felt it. As long as our planes fly overhead, the skies of America are free and that's what all of us everywhere are fighting for. And that we, in a very small way, are being allowed to help keep that sky free is the most beautiful thing I have ever known.

I, for one, am profoundly grateful that my one talent, my only knowledge, flying, happens to be of use to my country when it is needed. That's all the luck I ever hope to have."

* Flyer's Halo. A phenomenon familiar to flyers. The shadow of the plane on clouds, encircled from wing tip to wing tip by a complete rainbow.

NOTE: March 21, 1943, near Abilene, Texas while ferrying a BT-13 she lost her life in a mid-air collision. In Nashville, Tennessee, an airpark is named in her honor, Cornelia Fort Airpark. I find it ironic that Cornelia, who was almost killed while flying December 7, 1941, near Pearl Harbor, came back to the United States to fly for her country, only to become the first WASP to be killed. It seems she was destined to die while doing what she loved so much–flying.

## More Experiences Revealed

We had been so scattered during service that we had little knowledge of each other's activities. Later, as president of the WASP I had occasion to communicate with many members and learned so much about their varied experiences.

Elizabeth MacKethan Magid, who had never written a poem before, penned this poem "Celestial Flight" in memory of her friend Marie Michell Robinson.

# CELESTIAL FLIGHT

She is not dead –
But only flying higher,
Higher than she's flown before,
And earthly limitations
Will hinder her no more.

There is no service ceiling,
Or any fuel range,
And there is no anoxia,
Or need for engine change.
Thank God that now her flight can be
To heights her eyes had scanned,
Where she can race with comets,
And buzz the rainbow's span.

For she is universal
Like courage, love and hope,
And all free, sweet emotions
Of vast and godly scope.

And understand a pilot's Fate
Is not the thing she fears,
But rather sadness left behind,
Your heartbreak and your tears.

So all you loved ones, dry your eyes,
Yes, it is wrong that you should grieve,
For she would love your courage more,
And she would want you to believe
She is not dead.
You should have known
That she is only flying higher,
Higher than she's ever flown.

(Permission to reprint granted by author.)

161

# How The Poem Came To Be Written

Elizabeth MacKethan Magid and Marie Michell Robinson entered the September 1943 WASP class at Avenger Field, Sweetwater, Texas. They became very close friends during training and exchanged a promise that if anything ever happened to one, the other would go to be with the bereaved mother, never really believing this promise would have to be kept.

After graduation from flight school in 1944 Elizabeth and Marie were stationed together as ferry pilots with the Air Transport Command at Love Field, Dallas, Texas. Later they were separated when Elizabeth was sent to Cochran Field, Georgia, where she flew overhauled basic and advanced trainers. Marie was sent to Victorville Air Force Base, California, where she flew twin-engine bombers. In October 1944 Marie was killed in the crash of a B-25. She was nineteen years old.

Before leaving for the memorial service Elizabeth completed her test flying duties for the day. As she soared upward amidst the soft fair-weather cumulus clouds, she fantasized that her friend was there. She recalled the happy days in training when she, Marie and sky were one–on playful silver wings. But Marie was not there any longer. Elizabeth landed and in a secluded spot in the operations room she penned "Celestial Flight" in words that seemed to come from a source other than herself.

As soon as possible, Elizabeth caught a military flight to Michigan and shared the words of the poem with Marie's mother, thus fulfilling the promise exchanged many months before on a dusty, windswept training field in Texas.

## WASP Reunion -September 1978
## Colorado Springs

This was the last reunion at which I served as president. At our business meeting Colonel Bruce Arnold gave his final Militarization Committee report reviewing what had been accomplished since 1975.

Excerpts from Colonel Bruce Arnold's report:

"The Chairmen of both Veterans Committees signed written promises that hearings would be held early in the first session of the next Congress–1977. Now was the time to really hit Congress with as much publicity as possible. As an indication of what a good job the WASP did in this respect, I was asked several times during 1977 the name of the public relations firm we had engaged and how much it was costing us. (We had none.) The Washington press contacted me for details. This was the break we had been waiting for and we acted accordingly. This was the status of things when we assembled at Hot Springs, Arkansas, later in the month. The press was there in force. It was great publicity with which to start off our big push for 1977. WASP all over the country started working on grass roots publicity. Petitions were started, local radio and TV stations were contacted, and interviews were made with local papers. We, the members of the Militarization Committee, wish to take this opportunity to thank all WASP and all members of the Fifinella Organization for the wonderful assistance they gave us. I personally wish to thank Bee Haydu for being an outstanding president and a perfect person for me to work with on this project. I couldn't have asked for a better leader."

It was very gratifying to hear his words of praise after all the work that our committees and the membership had done over the past three years.

## Senator Goldwater

Senator Goldwater was a generous man who was committed to helping the WASP. We wanted to do something for him and contacted his aide, Terry Emerson, who had also been extremely helpful, asking him if he could suggest something we might present to the Senator. He conferred with Goldwater and responded that the only thing the Senator wanted was to be able to address us at our next reunion. That was this reunion September 1978 at Colorado Springs. The Senator flew from Washington, D.C. in his own airplane the afternoon of September 30th, spoke at our banquet and although we had made arrangements for him to stay at the hotel, he flew back to Washington the same night because he had appointments the next day in D.C.

*Senator Goldwater lending Bee his glasses so she can read the inscription on the award we gave him. It is a small statue of Fifinella crafted by WASP sculptress, Ann Atkeison. The inscription reads:*

## Senator Barry Goldwater
## Champion of the Women Airforce Service Pilots
## WASP World War II for his efforts to obtain military
## veterans recognition.

*September 30, 1978 prior to WASP reunion banquet, Senator Barry Goldwater, Barbara and Bruce Arnold.*

*Joe and Bee Haydu with the Senator.*

# Excerpts from Bee Haydu's Report

"In compiling the President's Report and realizing it will be my last one I found it extremely difficult to try to summarize all that has been done. I looked about me in the spot in our New Jersey home I call 'office' at the boxes of WASP correspondence and other material. I looked on my desk at the unfinished personal business and thought of the many hours I had been working on WASP business instead of helping my family members with their various projects. As my eyes came back into focus on those boxes of correspondence, I was considering how I could tell you about the volumes I have written in connection with the office of president and work on the Militarization Committee since Reno in June 1975. Of course, I could have counted all the letters written but that would have been too time consuming. What I did instead was take the bathroom scale and weigh the boxes of WASP files. They weighed 63 pounds! We produced five newsletters in these past three and a half years, material for which had to be gathered. Letters of invitation as well as thank you notes and letters of condolence had to be written on a continuing basis.

As you know, Joe and I spend about six months in Florida and six months in New Jersey. In Florida I managed to get the use of a WATS line two evenings a week. This saved us a great deal of money and meant I could follow up on many details concerning militarization and organization business by phone. In New Jersey it's a different story. There I am in the country and about eight miles from the nearest town. It's a long trip to have anything Xeroxed or mailed quickly.

In reviewing the publicity for the fight, I estimated that I took part in the following:

Nine newspaper interviews–one of which was a syndicated UPI column that went to over 600 newspapers.

Eleven TV Interviews including "Good Morning America" and "To Tell The Truth."

Eight radio interviews–the UPI one went to more than 900 stations.

Six publications and magazines.

Nine personal appearances–talks, petition gathering, air shows, etc.

Four 'tried and failed'–one for the "Today Show".

I traveled frequently to Washington, D.C. to attend militarization strategy meetings under the leadership of Colonel Arnold–some with Senator Barry Goldwater and other congressmen and congresswomen.

In my files which are now with Texas Woman's University. Denton, Texas there is a file entitled "Publicity". It lists the states where publicity was given and the number of articles. Synopsis: 303 newspaper articles from 43 states, Canada, Guam, plus 30 publications that went nationwide.

I cannot emphasize strongly enough how fortunate we were to have Bruce Arnold as our leader. Without him this never would have been accomplished. Just before the May 1977 Senate Hearings I spent two weeks in Washington helping at our headquarters office, setting up filing systems, meeting with the Militarization Committee and those in the government, visiting senators, congressmen/women or their aides and preparing for the Senate Hearings. While there I worked late at night as well as Saturdays and Sundays. Over my term in office I estimate I spent at least thirty days in Washington.

In conclusion, I want you all to know that while this has been a lot of work, it was well worth it. I have made so many new, true friends, have met numerous interesting people, and have experienced many new things in my life. It has been a pleasure being the president of such a unique group of women whose many accomplishments other than that of having been a WASP are incredible and inspiring. I thank you from the bottom of my heart for the opportunity of serving you."

**We all celebrated when we were finally recognized as veterans of World War II–especially Joe, Joey, Steve and Diana!**

# FIFTEEN

# LOOKING BACK

When I asked my family and friends to comment on their recollections of our flying days I didn't know quite what to expect. Their comments brought back a flood of memories that I hope you enjoy reading.

### Lloyd Falk

When I learned my sister, Bernice, was learning to fly military aircraft, I was really amazed and proud of her. But I was not totally surprised because she was always an innovator and in the vanguard of breaking away from stereotypical women's work.

All the time she was doing this, I was in the Army Air Force in the United States, England and later, France. I had been trained by the Army to be a meteorologist and eventually was assigned to the group in England who prepared weather forecasts for General Eisenhower's staff. We were actively involved in the weather forecast for the D-day invasion of France. While I was in Europe, both Bee and our mother kept me informed of her WASP activities and adventures.

By the time I returned home in 1945, unfortunately the WASP had already been disbanded. But Bee's activities over the years on behalf of the WASP have always been of immense interest to both my wife, Eleanor, and me. We especially admired her tenacity and ability in leading the group to their goal of procuring military status.

Eleanor and I have three children, David, Laurie and Gary and four grandchildren. We enjoy retired life and the many activities with which it is associated.

NOTE: Eleanor and Lloyd were married when he returned from service in 1945. We had known Eleanor and her family and were friends throughout most of our school years. She has always been a dear friend putting her family before all else. After the war Lloyd returned to academic life at Rutgers University and obtained a Ph.D. in environmental science in 1949. He then joined the Du Pont Company's Engineering Department where he became involved in many aspects of air and water pollution control until his retirement in 1981 after thirty-two years.

## Jacqueline Falk Menard

I was between ten and eleven years old and in the 5th or 6th grade during World War II. My brother was in the Army Air Force as a meteorologist. We lived in East Orange, New Jersey and my sister, Bernice, who worked as a secretary, started taking flying lessons in Pennsylvania.

I remember going to where she was learning to fly and her instructor took me for a ride in one of the planes. He let me take the controls and actually allowed me to log a half-hour of instruction. I wasn't afraid. I loved flying and still do–I guess it's in our blood.

When my sister joined the WASP, we had a small flag in the window with two stars, one each for my brother and sister (that was the custom if you had any family members in the services). Since my siblings were so much older than I, none of my friends had brothers and certainly it was not usual to have a sister who flew airplanes. My family's attitude was that women could be or do anything they wanted. I remember being very proud and not being afraid about them in the war. Any fear my parents may have had was never passed on to me and I was a bit young to really understand the dangers.

Both my brother and sister wrote letters to me and I wrote back. Since my brother, Lloyd, was in England we had to use v-mail. They were on special paper that would then be photographed and reduced in size to be sent overseas. I remember Bee sending me a colored picture of Fifinella. I showed this to my friends and made my own copy which I sent to her.

In the summer of 1944 when I was almost 12, my mother and I took a Greyhound bus trip from New Jersey all the way to California and then to Sweetwater, Texas, to my sister's graduation. I remember the barracks they lived in and taking a shower there with my big sister. We attended the graduation and saw Bee get her Wings. It was indeed a proud moment. All in all, I loved being a part of this. For a kid my age it was such a wonderful opportunity to travel and expand my world.

As an adult, I have been bragging about my sister to all who will listen. Seeing there had been no mention of the WASP in the Smithsonian Air & Space Museum, she called this to their attention, donated her WASP uniform, which is on display, and gave them pictures along with a great deal of information. When she was president of the WASP, her leadership and hard work helped achieve success in obtaining veteran status for the women who served in the WASP.

NOTE: Jacqueline (now Jacki) graduated from Parsons School of Design in New York City and became an interior designer. Her lovely home exhibits her excellent taste. She has three wonderful children, Greta, Vivian and Neil, and two granddaughters. Since she is semi-retired from designing, she now works using her acquired computer skills. She and her husband David (a mergers and acquisitions broker) live in Villanova, Pennsylvania. I shall always cherish my 'little sister.'

We asked our wonderful children what it felt like growing up in an aviation oriented family. Here is what they said:

### Joseph D. Haydu

Cessna 172, 210, 310, Stearman, T-38, Link trainer–on the side porch! Air shows, 'hangar flying', waxing the airplane, 'touch and goes'*. These are all things I remember as a young boy growing up in a flying family.

Probably one of the most exceptional memories was learning to fly a PT-17 Stearman at the ripe age of twelve. My father, being an Army Primary Instructor during World War II, taught me the 'Army Way'. S turns, steep 360 degree turns, straight and level–"Keep the horizon level with the air intake" and so on**. A picture of a Stearman, which looks like N179M hangs on a wall in my home today. As a twelve year old, I took this for granted, but as an adult I cherish the experience.

In addition to being an accomplished pilot, navigation was my Mom's thing. I was in the 6th grade and she was showing me how to do some basic function with the E6B computer. She said, "Now you can tell your teacher that you know how to work a computer." For those of you who don't know what an E6B computer is, it's a mechanical circular device with no batteries, no display, no hard drive and is not anything like today's modern personal computers. It is an aviator's equivalent to an engineer's slide rule. Maybe this is what got me started in computers?

And then there were the cross-country trips. Niagara Falls to see the falls and be home the same day. I have a picture on my wall with all of us dressed in the yellow rain coats that you wear when you go under the falls. Atlantic City–just to walk the boardwalk and play a few wheels. Flying W Ranch in South Jersey because they had good hamburgers and Haydu hot dogs. Wilkes Barre Airport in Pennsylvania to shoot ILS*** approaches. A ride in the Goodyear blimp–Mom got to fly. To us this was just another day out. But to our friends this was awesome.

To this day, I still use the lessons learned from flying. I hear my mother saying, "When you are lost, the first thing you do is fly the airplane on your planned heading." Or my father's favorite, "When in doubt–NO!" or, "Look out for the other guy." Simple sayings that can save your life and are applicable for a car, boat, bicycle, golf cart or anything else you might drive, pilot or ride.

Well, I've certainly enjoyed writing this for my Mom's book. It brings back fond memories and makes me appreciate the great flying experiences I've been fortunate enough to have. But mostly it's how wonderful both my parents have been to me and my brother and sister. Best wishes on your book, Busy.**** Your son, Joe

*When a student pilot reaches the takeoffs and landings portion of his training, he takes off, flies the traffic pattern, lands and then immediately puts in full throttle to takeoff again for another practice round. The student is able to practice more takeoffs and landings with this method.

**Joe's references to what he did while learning to fly are maneuvers performed by student pilots when practicing.

***The ILS (instrument landing system) approaches are facilities on the ground that give signals to an instrument in the plane to aid the pilot landing under instrument conditions.

****Joe gave me the name 'Busy Bee' since it seemed I was always busy.

NOTE: Joe is an licensed real estate appraiser in the state of New Jersey. He is also a Microsoft Certified Systems Engineer. He lives in Florham Park, N. J. and is a Real Estate Review Appraiser for a major financial institution.


## Steven Haydu


Growing up in a flying family was always fun and exciting. I remember one time when I flew with my Mom. I was really young at the time and it was a thrill for me to sit up front in the right seat. It was a high wing airplane and I had a great view of the world below. My Mom took it off, got to altitude and leveled off, then said, "Here, you take it." So I took the controls and pulled myself up to get closer to the controls. The yoke came back, the nose went up, the ground disappeared and the sky got really big in the windshield. Then I felt a push on the yoke. Of course, it was Mom and she said, "Try again," which I did. I enjoyed myself that day and whenever the front seat became available, I was first in line.

My father was a flight instructor in World War II in an open cockpit, tandem* two seater Stearman plane. He served for three and a half years and was an extremely proficient commercial pilot with his instructor's rating. He had a lot of hours flying. The first airplane I recall our owning was a restored Stearman. Pop gave me some lessons but I was too young and small to really be able to fly what was to me a large airplane.

In later years when I was older and larger my parents gave all of us flying lessons through a flying club. It was then I acquired about forty hours of flying time. Some time after college I finished my pilot training and earned my private pilot's license. I believe it was those fond memories of flying that helped motivate me to fly. It's funny, now when I'm outside with Mom or Pop and we hear a plane over head, we look up and think about flying. Once you've had the flight experience, it never leaves you. I know that and so do Mom and Pop. Now whenever I have an opportunity to fly with Mom she always says, "Steve, you fly and I'll work the radios." I love that, I love flying and I love my Mom and Pop.


*Tandem seating is when one person sits behind the other rather than side by side.

NOTE: Karla, Steve's wife, married into this 'aviation crazy' family in 1986 and has been an enthusiastic supporter to all of us. How fortunate we are to have such a wonderful, understanding family. Steve owned airplanes and continued to fly until his children were born. He is an excellent pilot and I'm sure will go back to it some day. At one time Steve owned a restaurant called Country Farms in Blairstown, New Jersey. He now owns and operates a painting contractor business in the Hackettstown, New Jersey area. Karla works for Master Foods USA as a finance specialist. They and their two daughters, Sara and Christina, live in Allamuchy, New Jersey.

Our two youngest granddaughters wanted to say something.


### Sara and Christina Haydu


We were too young to be included in the many flying activities. But we remember Grandma showing us pictures of Fifinella and teaching us how to say her name. She told us many stories of flying. My mother and father speak often about the fun of flying. Maybe someday we will learn to fly.

NOTE: Sara is sixteen and in the 11th grade. Christina is fifteen and in the 9th grade. Two lovable grand-daughters.


### Diana Haydu Potter


Growing up in a family dominated by aviation was always exciting. Summers were spent under the wing of an airplane at the many shows. Winters were dedicated to washing the airplane in the hangar. Since I was the youngest and smallest, my job was to keep the landing gear clean. Somehow I never grew out of that job. My favorite plane was a Boeing Stearman. I loved the freedom of an open cockpit, of really feeling the plane when you flew, listening to the engine whine during stunts, being cold upstairs and hot on the ground. The most memorable Christmas I ever had was when Mom and Pop gave us a children's parachute so we could go stunt flying with them. That was truly seat-of-your-pants flying!* It helped me understand why my folks were so passionate about the sport. I do recall one time when we had the Link trainer on the porch, Steve and I, unsupervised, were using it. There is a desk next to the Link on which there is a stylus that records what you are doing in the Link. Well, we were so absorbed in what was going on in the Link, we did not notice until too late that the stylus had worked its way completely off the desk–CRASH! We quickly put it back on the desk and said nothing. I guess now our parents know why they had to have the repairman in again.

Throughout all the planes and all the races and flights, open cockpit flying remains my personal favorite. To this day, I look up when I hear a radial engine. When I walk through a small airport and smell that hangar smell, I recall an entire childhood. Life was fun!

*Seat-of-your-pants flying refers to the feeling a pilot learns. No matter in what position the plane might be, you must feel as if you are a part of the plane. For example, if you are making a bank (turn), lean with the bank, not away from it.

NOTE: Diana is not only a good daughter but a good friend. We really enjoy each other's company and seem to have the same sense of humor. As of this writing, Diana is with Novartis Pharmaceuticals Corporation and travels worldwide supporting cancer research. Her impressive title is Global Head, Oncology Scientific Operations.

### Jeffrey Potter

When Diana Haydu and I were dating, she was going to college in Tampa where we met. My now in-laws would fly their Beech Bonanza airplane to McKnight field in the Tampa area, pick up Diana and me and fly us to their condominium in Palm Beach Gardens for the weekend. During one of these trips when Bee was flying and I was in the copilot's seat, she gave me the controls of the airplane and let me fly. This was an exciting experience for me. After Diana and I were married, I earned my pilot's license. When our lives became busy with children and business, I gave up flying but fully intend to some day return. Both my in-laws are excellent pilots and have shared so much with all of us. Through the years we have spent vacations together, always having fun. Their sense of humor and willingness to have fun makes them wonderful to be around.

NOTE: Jeffrey is a real estate investor. He and Diana owned many properties in Richmond, Texas. Jeff is a very special member of our family. He is always considerate and has a knack for anticipating the needs of others.

Since our two older granddaughters had participated in many of the WASP functions, we wanted their opinions.


## Katheryn Potter

I will always remember my grandma as a very strong willed woman. Growing up and going to WASP reunions and functions, Grandma has made me so proud. It's not just me, it's all the women who have died fighting for what they believed in and it's all the children who look up to my grandma for what she has accomplished. I see Grandma as a role model for people everywhere. I remember when I was in the 4th grade and Grandma and Grandpa came to talk to my class about airplanes. The kids thought that was the coolest thing and for about a week they all thought they were pilots. Some of my friends look back and still remember my grandparents to this day. Grandpa was a great athlete. He played baseball and when he graduated from high school in 1935, the New York Giants baseball team recruited him.

In the war they weren't allowing women to join the Air Force. In later years Grandma was one of the women who fought against this and successfully helped them and others spread their wings in the military. Not only has she had a huge success in her career, but a huge success in life. The most wonderful man in the world, Joseph Haydu, Grandpa, has supported Grandma in everything she has done. They have two very successful sons and a daughter and four great grandkids. Basically Grandma's life seems like a dream.

NOTE: In January 13, 2010, Katheryn, graduated from Hawaii Pacitic University at the age of 23. She works in Houston, Texas as an adminstration assistant for Moody Rambin Interests. She is a bright young lady capable of achieving anything to which she sets her mind.

I was only five years old then so I do not remember all the details. There was a WASP reunion in Sweetwater, Texas. We lived in Richmond, Texas, and Grandma and Grandpa were taking care of us while my parents were in France on a business trip. Grandpa taught us how to play checkers, while Grandma was cooking. He was really good!

We drove to Sweetwater to meet other members of the family who were coming to the reunion. The WASP had a room where they all got together and my sister, Katheryn, and I would stand outside the room, hold the door open for them and salute them. Grandma had taught us how to salute and had made each of us a uniform on the back of which it said, 'My Grandma Flew in World War II.' A few months later we went to Midland, Texas, with my parents and met my grandparents there. Senator Barry Goldwater was the speaker at a luncheon. My parents told me Senator Goldwater was a very important person and had run for president of the United States. Grandma had made an album of things he had done for the WASP for us to give him. I remember all of us being photographed with Senator Goldwater and I have an autographed picture of that day. In school we studied the history of those times and of the people who were there. To meet them was inspirational and to think Grandma was one of the pioneers of history is amazing.

Caring, loving, comforting, supporting–there are not enough words to describe my grandmother. The joy she has brought to us is indescribable. She may say we have enriched her life but she has helped to shape and mold mine. When I was younger I was never able to grasp her accomplishments. I only knew her as my grandmother but with coming of age, I can now understand and respect her not only as my grandmother but also as a woman who did something with her life.

NOTE: Kristen, now twtenty-two, graduated Texas Wesleyan University, Fort Worth, Texas, majoring in marketing, May 14, 2010. She has received a scholarship for her accomplishments as a pianist and has made the Dean's list. Kristen is an excellent student who perseveres. She will succeed at anything she undertakes.

# COMMENTS FROM SOME OF THE WASP

## Gerry Ashwell Lotowycz

What fun we had learning to fly together at Martins Creek, Pennsylvania, before being accepted into the WASP program. I wanted to do something because of the war. Everyone wanted to do something. My uncle had been a pilot in World War I and he inspired me to become a pilot. I lived in Connecticut and we could not fly along the East Coast, which led me to Martins Creek for flying lessons. During our training there were six of us who had gone together for the WASP class of 44-7. We encouraged each other through many troubling times–especially when three of the six did not make it. Prior to learning to fly I was employed as a curatorial assistant at the Brooklyn Botanical Gardens. While learning to fly I worked in the *Life* magazine letters department answering letters from the public about articles in the magazine. After the WASP were disbanded I had an idea for a business that would allow me to continue flying. To insure their freshness there was a need to transport lobsters from Maine to the New York metropolitan area as quickly as possible. I wanted to be the one to fly them there. I diligently studied lobsters learning all I could about them including their sex lives and how they might react to altitude. The reason this venture did not come into fruition was that the high-winged monoplane I was going to use caught fire and burned. I also applied for a job as a pilot with American Airlines. With the name 'Gerry,' they invited me for an interview. But when the man in the hiring department saw me, he was amazed to see I was a woman. He took me to meet the vice president in charge of the department. At that time people were not afraid of being sued for discrimination. The vice president was very polite but said he did not think the flying public was ready yet for women pilots. He offered me a job as a stewardess, which I refused.

Eventually, I went back to my original career as a botanist. An arboretum had opened up only a mile from my home in Oyster Bay, New York and I worked there until I retired. Flying and the WASP provided some of the most outstanding experiences of my life. Bee and I have shared so many great times together!

NOTE: Gerry married Bill Lotowycz in 1946. They had four daughters.

Unfortunately Bill died in 1982. Although we do not see each other often, we have kept in touch all these years. Currently Gerry lives in Boulder, Colorado, close to her oldest and youngest daughters.

## Elizabeth "Betty" Pettitt Nicholas

Unfortunately Betty died February 6, 1998. We learned to fly together at Martins Creek, Pennsylvania and were in the same class at Avenger Field, Sweetwater, Texas. After the WASP disbanded Betty ferried aircraft including ferrying for the company I owned. She eventually got a position in Indianapolis, Indiana as a skywriter. She performed these tasks in an AT-6 and was the first woman in Indiana to do that type of work. While working in Indianapolis she met Ted Nicholas whom she married. When I was the president of the WASP organization, Betty was the secretary/treasurer and did a tremendous amount of work in that position. She continued being active in the WASP. She was a good, true friend and is sadly missed.

## Alice Gartland Whitmore

I was proud to have qualified for the WASP training program–it was very challenging. I felt sorry that I did not complete the program and to this day do not know what trick of fate caused that. Prior to WASP training I was working at Handy & Harmon as a secretary. During that time I was learning to fly at Martins Creek, Pennsylvania where I met Bee. This is where a life-long friendship began. In our single days, we would spend summer vacations together, always fun times. When I left WASP training, I returned to Long Island. In 1951 I met Michael Whitmore and we were married in 1952. We had two girls and two boys, all of whom I am so proud. Unfortunately Michael died of cancer in 1990. After raising our family I worked for Port Washington Credit Union as a loan officer for over ten years. It has been a good life.

NOTE: Alice has always been a special friend. Although we have not had occasion to be together often over the years, when we do meet, it is as if we had seen each other just yesterday and we pick up the conversation from there. Alice currently resides in Glen Cove, Long Island, New York.

# Sara Payne Hayden

In 1975 I was elected vice president of the WASP organization. We had never had a vice president before and so my duties were vague. I felt I needed something to do and thought it would be good to bring organization to the various items individual members had for sale. Our meager treasury was barely sufficient to cover the cost of newsletters and rosters. We also had to consider the expenses we would be incurring in the political struggle we were about to encounter. With the enthusiastic agreement of our board I set up our 'store' adding WASP memorabilia items. We had manufacturers make many jewelry items including replicas of our wings, which up until now had not been available to buy or replace. Other items we had manufactured were t-shirts, stationery, decals, etc. Some members created Fifinella needlework, pillows and wrote books. The cooperation I received was fantastic including help in the salesrooms at reunions. We conducted stores at the Hot Springs 1976 reunion and the Colorado Springs 1978 reunion. I was completely surprised and overwhelmed at the response. We added in excess of $20,000 to the treasury plus turning over a large inventory to the next board. Currently Florence "Shutsy" Reynolds is operating the store. She has expanded the stock immensely and is always adding new items. Her capable management has added a great deal of money to the treasury.

Our board worked so well together that we formed a permanent bond, which has not dimmed. Bee led the way in teaching us that we could disagree, shoot down ideas without incurring hard feelings, and always work for the good of our organization.

After we were disbanded I earned my commercial license and flight instructor's rating, continuing to fly. I was commissioned as a 2nd Lt. in the United States Air Force Reserve in 1949 and called to active duty in 1951 as a recruiter. I have served as an officer in the New England Section and Eastern New England Chapter of the Ninety-Nines and as Commander of the American Legion Methuen Women's Post 417. Currently I am the WASP veterans affairs person giving assistance to members regarding their rights, the paperwork necessary and alerting them of any changes in any veterans affairs that might concern them.

NOTE: Sara married Frank Hayden, M.D. in 1953. He had been with the

Armed Forces Examining Station in Nashville, Tennessee, one of the places Sara had been assigned. He is currently retired. They have two children–one followed in Dad's footsteps and is a doctor. They live in Methuen, Massachusetts. Sara was an extremely valuable asset to our board, always willing to take on more than her share.

## Mary "Marty" Martin Wyall

When I was elected as a board member of the WASP organization in 1975, I had no idea there would be so much information necessary for our struggle to be recognized as veterans of World War II. I lived on a farm and had been collecting items from the WASP for years. A great deal of this information was used in our 'battle' in Washington, D.C. During those financially lean years we were always aware of the need to be frugal. Consequently, when our board met, we would travel at our own expense, eat and stay with other WASP to save hotel expenses. It was a pleasure serving with the elected board—all of them worked diligently for the organization. Some years later, as historian for the WASP, I helped select the Texas Woman's University, Denton, Texas, as the archivist of all WASP memorabilia. My collection has been given to them.

It was fun working with Bee and the proof of that is, we are still good friends. After we were disbanded I ferried surplus aircraft and obtained my instructor's rating. Gene Wyall, was one of my students. We married in January 1946 and raised a family of four boys and one girl. Gene was a civil engineer in heavy construction projects. He worked for other highway contractors as general superintendent until he formed his own company, Maumee Construction. In 1965 because of a need for speedy transportation of parts and/or personnel, he convinced me to go back to flying. In 1966 I was the first and only woman to operate a passenger/freight service in Indiana under the FAA Air Taxi Certificate #135. Eventually it became too expensive to maintain the air taxi certificate.

NOTE: After flying for their company, Marty continued to fly, free lancing for large corporations. She stopped piloting in 1979. Gene died July 1993. Marty is a wealth of information and has been a great asset to the WASP organization.

## Eleanor Gunderson

During our seven months training I was Bee Falk's bay mate at Avenger Field. Now you would think that six young women in a small area over a period of time might not get along together all of the time. Actually, I can't recall any of the six of us ever having an argument. I had the reputation of being, shall we say, 'not so neat'. Every Saturday we had SMI (Saturday morning inspection) and if ANYTHING was out of place–like trash in the wastebasket, water in the sink–we would all get demerits. Enough demerits and we would not be allowed off the base on our day off. So you can see that I sometimes made my friends nervous and consequently they always gave me a helping hand on Saturdays. (Not a bad strategy.) I recall when one of our bay mates obtained a copy of Edgar Allen Poe's "The Cask of Amontillado." It was after bed check. We all sat on the floor reading it by candlelight. We probably got to where the guy was about to be buried alive when a gust of wind blew out the candle. We all scrambled into our beds–BRAVE, INTREPID WORLD WAR II PILOTS!! Another time four of us decided to shoot craps in the latrine–after bed check, of course. We always took a Bible with us in case we were caught. Who could demerit us for reading the Bible in the latrine after hours??? All in all it was the most exciting experience of my life.

NOTE: Eleanor is a talented artist who drew the many cartoons for our class yearbook. After we were disbanded she joined the Air Force Reserves where she served for ten years. She then became an air traffic controller. She went to the University of Arizona to continue art studies and helped them set up their visual aids. She does free lance art work in addition to being an extra in such TV series as *The Gilmore Girls, Scrubs* and many others. She has one son. There is no stopping this woman.

## Betty Jane Williams

I have always been active in the WASP organization and was their second president, serving two terms from 1947 through 1949. In 1975 I was living in California when asked to assist in the promotion of our desire to obtain military status. The most important group that nationally did not support the WASP, although some state chapters did, was the American Legion. Bruce Arnold asked me to go to their national convention where the WASP legislation was to be discussed. There were a good half dozen WASP there and they asked me to be the spokesperson. I wore my Air Force uniform to show it was not a personal issue with me since I was already actively involved in the Air Force. Unfortunately the National American Legion was rude to the group of WASP as a whole and outwardly expressed their negative attitude about our trying to be recognized by our government. The outcome of our request at that meeting was to have the subject moved to committee, which is a tricky way to 'kill it.' The disturbing thing was that the Air Force Association and the Air Force Reserves had given their support. Most of my life after the WASP were disbanded I was connected with publicity enabling me to procure the much needed exposure during this time.

NOTE: After we were disbanded Betty Jane Williams obtained her instructor's rating and continued to fly. She pioneered in the use of TV to acquaint the public with aviation over CBS and NBC, in New York. She joined the Army Air Force Reserves and was called to active duty during the Korean War as a TV writer-producer and remained active in the Reserves for twenty-eight years. She wrote flight operations handbooks and produced information films for both North American Aviation and Lockheed. She also had her own film TV company for several years.

### Betty Tackaberry Blake

In 1941 I was flying tourists around Oahu and between the islands in open cockpit biplanes for Andrew Flying Service at John Rodgers Airport in Hawaii (now Honolulu International) located right beside Hickam Field and Pearl Harbor. Cornelia Fort was also a flight instructor there. As an instructor she was flying an Interstate Cadet, which replaced the previously used Piper Cubs. She was flying with a student who was practicing takeoffs and landings on December 7, 1941, when the Japanese invaded by air. They shot her airplane. I saw it the next day and there were bullet holes in the wings fortunately missing the gas tanks. I had been scheduled to fly tourists that fatal day but the flight was cancelled–lucky for me.

As soon as we could, Cornelia and I returned to the United States. Cornelia joined the Women's Auxiliary Ferrying Service under Nancy Love, which group later became the WASP. I entered the first class of the Women's Flying Training Detachment, which also later became the WASP. While in service with the WASP I flew all the fighter aircraft and also the B-25, B-26, B-17 bombers and the C-47 cargo aircraft as well as all the trainers. When stationed in Long Beach, California, I met Air Force Captain George W. Blake III. He operated the airlines at the base and I was nice to him, since he assigned the crews, and I wanted to fly four-engine aircraft. It got to be a habit and we were married in Phoenix, Arizona, in May 1946. We had three sons, all pilots, the youngest an airline pilot. After we were disbanded I became a Link trainer instructor. I also flew shrimp from New Orleans to Los Angeles in a twin engine Cessna. So far it's been a GREAT ride with a busy Guardian Angel at my side.

NOTE: Betty's achievements were varied. For five years she wrote a newspaper gossip column for *The Scottsdale Progress*. They also manufactured stuffed animals and made a frog that Jack Lemon used as a love symbol in his movie *April Fools*. Then she became continuity director for station KPHO in Phoenix. An extremely accomplished lady–typical of so many WASP.

## Stearman N179M

My name was November 179Mike and I was a very famous airplane. Not only did I win many trophies for being the best restored but I was used in many advertisements. I was really beautiful in my original colors of blue and yellow with a red and white striped tail. I was born sometime in 1943, the 293rd of a unit of 658 planes. Boeing Aircraft in Wichita, Kansas, gave me the formal name of Boeing Kaydet but my friends call me PT-17 or Stearman (designed by Lloyd Stearman in 1935). There were 8,584 of us built during World War II. My brothers and sisters and I trained more than 60,000 military pilots in World War II. In 1964 Boeing said "Most of us feel that the Kaydet has more personality than the big machines we are working on now."

After the war I was declared surplus and a United Airlines copilot, Robert Lewis, purchased me with the thought of rebuilding me. Unfortunately he was killed in 1962 in Washington, D.C. in the United Viscount crash. His father wanting Robert's ambition realized went to his friend, Graham Denham in Millville, New Jersey, requesting that he fulfill this dream. This Denham did with skill and love for every detail. In 1963 Joe and Bee Haydu and their three children became my new family.

*1966—This was a luggage ad. The man holding the suitcase is Orson Beane, a famous actor and one of the November 1977 "To Tell The Truth" panel.*

Remember when tape <u>only</u> held things down?

The sky's the limit with modern Mystik tapes from Borden Chemical!

*1966 –The man putting the tape on me is my owner, Joe Haydu.*

183

# Tom Reilly's Flying Tigers Warbird Restoration Museum, Kissimmee, Florida

## November 2002–WASP were given rides in the AT-6 and B-25 and allowed to fly, once airborne.

*Barry Smith, Norma Halberg, Nonie Anderson, Kaddy Steele, Bee Haydu and Shirley Kruse standing in front of the B-25.*

*July 26, 2010. For a short time Bee was at the controls of DC3 HERPA, owned by Dan Gryder. We were the lead ship of a formation of 23 DC3 and C47 aircraft flying from Sterling, IL to Oshkock, WI for the 75th Anniversary of the DC3. Of course, Dan actually flew most of the trip including take off and landing.*

# SIXTEEN

## SUMMING UP

The WASP organization continues to meet every two years. The 50th reunion in May 1993 took place in Sweetwater, Texas, at Avenger Field where we had been trained. The Wishing Well into which we had thrown our coins for good luck had been restored. A new plaque to replace the one General Arnold had given us (which had been stolen) was installed. A statue of a WASP, face uplifted, eyes looking skyward, was placed in the center of the Wishing Well. It had been crafted and donated by Dorothy Lewis, a WASP who is a renowned sculptress. The Sweetwater, Texas, Chamber of Commerce had solicited donations and had erected a Wall of Honor inscribed with the names of all the WASP.

On this occasion the two main speakers were United States Attorney General Janet Reno, niece of WASP Winifred Wood, and Texas Governor Ann Richards. Our family, Joe and Cozette; Steve and Karla, and two granddaughters Katheryn and Kristen Potter attended. Our daughter and

*Kristen (5) and Katheryn (6) looking for Grandma's name on the wall in the Walk of Honor. They are wearing the 'uniforms' made by Grandma complete with miniature WASP wings and black neckties. The back of their shirts read, "My Grandma Flew in World War II".*

son-in-law were in France at the time and our two other granddaughters had not been born.

Our children were amazed at the velocity of the wind. They could not believe that we were taught to fly under such windy conditions. (A northerly wind blew at a constant twenty-five miles per hour at Avenger Field.) It made me think back about being instructed in cross-wind takeoffs and landings. The wind rarely blows directly down a runway, therefore, one has to become proficient at taking off and landing with a cross-wind. Planes with a narrow landing gear were more difficult to maneuver in the cross-wind. The Stearman aircraft was chosen for primary training because it had a narrower landing gear than other trainers and would help prepare us for the next aircraft we would be flying–the AT-6, which also has a narrow landing gear.

If the children thought the wind strong at Sweetwater, they should visit Pecos, Texas, where I was stationed and where the wind blew at an even higher velocity.

*May 1993–seated Steven and Kristen on his lap, Karla with Katheryn. Standing Bee and Joe Haydu, Cozette, and Joseph.*

<u>Senator Barry Goldwater</u>

In November 1993 the American Airpower Heritage Museum at the Confederate Air Force Headquarters, Midland, Texas, hosted a symposium on World War II. When we learned that Senator Barry Goldwater was to be the guest speaker, we contacted our daughter Diana and her husband Jeff (who live in Richmond, Texas) asking them to meet us there with our granddaughters, Katheryn and Kristen–in their uniforms. I assembled an album with pictures and items for the Senator, which depicted his involvement when he was doing so much for the WASP. After his speech the girls and I presented him with the album.

*November 12, 1993,
Midland, Texas–Jeff
and Diana Potter,
Joe and Bee Haydu,
Senator Goldwater,
Katheryn and
Kristen Potter.*

We then visited Avenger Field, Sweetwater, to show Diana and Jeff the restored Wishing Well, the Statue and the Walk of Honor.

*November 1993–
Katheryn, Bee and
Kristen at the
Wishing Well.*

*Karla and Steve's two girls,
Christina and Sara, would
have participated in some of
these activities but they had
not beenborn yet.  This is a
picture of these darling girls,
Christina, 12 and Sara 13.*

# A Proud Moment

In September 1999 I received a letter from Edmund Nelle, Jr., President of the Aviation Hall of Fame & Museum of New Jersey. It said in part:

"On behalf of our Board of Trustees, it gives me great pleasure to inform you of your unanimous election into the Aviation Hall of Fame & Museum of New Jersey. Our Trustees recognize your service to our nation as a WASP, your leadership in securing military benefits for those dedicated women who flew during World War II and your being among the first women in our State to create your own aviation business."

When I received this letter, I said to Joe, "I'm sure they must have the wrong person–but I'm not going to tell them".

The actual induction was on May 11, 2000, at which time I addressed the four hundred plus guests at the banquet held in the Fiesta Ballroom, Wood Ridge, New Jersey. Of course, all of our immediate family were there, as well as many friends.

*May 11, 2000, President Edmund Nelle, Jr. presenting Bee with the plaque that is now in the Aviation Hall of Fame.*

The inscription on the plaque reads:

## BERNICE FALK HAYDU
## WASP LEADER

Bernice Falk Haydu, a Bradley Beach, New Jersey native, took flying lessons in 1943 to acquire sufficient hours to qualify for training with the Women Airforce Service Pilots (WASP) at Sweetwater, Texas. Upon graduation from the Aviation Cadet Program, she served at Pecos Air Base,

Pecos, Texas, flying twin-engine aircraft as an engineering test pilot until the WASP disbanded in 1944.

Following the war, Mrs. Haydu formed Garden State Airways, a ferrying service for Aeronca and Cessna aircraft from the factory to the New York metropolitan area, and procured a Cessna dealership. She was then among just a handful of women aviation executives in the nation. In 1947, she and eight male veterans bought a flight school at Woodbridge Airport, Iselin, New Jersey, where she served as Director of Operations and was a flight instructor. When the Garden State Parkway construction ran through the airport's runway, it was closed in 1948. For more than a year, Mrs. Haydu fought the State Department of Transportation for her company's initial investment of $28,000 and won.

She took on a larger bureaucracy, the United States Government during her two terms as President of the WASP organization (1975-78). Although WASP wore uniforms, were trained and disciplined like their male Air Force counterparts, they were paid as Civil Service personnel. At the war's end, they were vaguely promised G.I. benefits that never materialized. Bee Haydu took their case to Washington and two years later, with the help of Col. Bruce Arnold and Senator Barry Goldwater, the WASP were granted military benefits.

Mrs. Haydu has flown in three Powder Puff Derbies, the 1965 Angel Derby and various air shows. She was instrumental in developing a permanent WASP exhibit at the Smithsonian's Air & Space Museum, Washington, DC.

Inducted Aviation Hall of Fame & Museum of New Jersey 2000.

## The Next Generations

In 1977 our board of directors wanted to include current women military pilots in the WASP organization. However, the majority of WASP voted to include only WASP. Therefore, we founded the Women Military Pilots, Inc. This organization is active and has a convention every other year. The name has been changed to Women Military Aviators, Inc. in order to include women graduates of military pilot and navigational training programs as well as women aircrew members as specified by each branch of the service and, of course, the WASP. Our current membership includes many notable pilots such as Eileen Collins, the first woman commander of a space shuttle and Barbara McConnell Barrett, newly appointed Secretary of the Air Force. It is a pleasure to meet these younger aviators and to become cognizant of their amazing accomplishments. I am proud to be their historian.

The History Channel was preparing a documentary called *WOMEN COMBAT PILOTS – The Right Stuff.* This first aired March 9, 2003, and is shown from time to time. Since the WASP are considered the pioneers of female military pilots, I was honored to be included in portions of the program.

## Aviation Airport Advisory Board

In 1984 I became a member of the Aviation Airport Advisory Board of Palm Beach County. We are appointed by the county commissioners, serving at their pleasure and report to them on activities in the four county-owned airports. We meet each month or as needed and had a great deal of input when the new Palm Beach Airport Terminal was constructed. We report to the county commissioners regarding matters involving the airports when we deem it necessary. The airports receive no funds from taxes and operate at a profit. In 2007 I resigned from AAAB after 23 years of service.

*February 28, 2001, we celebrated our*
*50th Wedding Anniversary.*

*Thanksgiving 2002–Family gathering–Joey and Cozette, Jeffrey & Diana, Joe, Katheryn\*, Bee, Kristen\*, Karla and Steve, Christina & Sara. \*Diana and Jeff's children the two who wore miniature 'uniforms' at Sweetwater in 1993.*

## ALL GOOD THINGS MUST COME TO AN END

Joe and I stopped flying as pilots in command in 1996. We have never lost interest in aviation and belong to many aviation related organizations and still attend many air shows.

The last airplane we owned was one of the most interesting. It was a YAK-52 N51114 manufactured in Russia. We purchased it in June 1993. This is a two place aerobatic training aircraft. It differs from those manufactured in the United States. The propeller rotates in the opposite direction and it is started by air pressure. Since hydraulic systems are not practical in the cold Russian climate the flaps and gear also operate by air. Once airborne, the air in the tank is replenished. If the plane is low on air when starting, there is an external outlet so more air can be put into the tanks by using an auxiliary source such as a scuba diving air tank. The engine still runs on gasoline. This was the last airplane we owned and after we sold it in 1995, we decided to retire from piloting.

Regarding my flying, I have been asked many times, "Would you do it again?" My response–

## "IN A HEARTBEAT!!!"

# AFTERWORD

The writing of this book has been a labor of love, not only of flying, but life. I have enjoyed recalling to mind all the wonderful experiences I have had growing up with aviation. As a young woman being accepted into the WASP, learning the discipline of flying, meeting all those bright, courageous, valiant, young women from all over the country, was exhilarating. It was an exciting time for aviation, and for women. Both were coming into their own.

Then meeting and marrying Joe, a beloved man, who shared my passion for flying and love of family–our three wonderful children–how lucky can you get?

Hopefully, this book will inspire the youth of today to aspire to lofty ambitions and realize that perseverance is the main ingredient in the recipe for success.

**The harder you work, the luckier you get!**

*Profits from this book will go to Texas Woman's University Foundation*

# EPILOGUE

## WASP RECEIVE CONGRESSIONAL GOLD MEDAL

In 1977 I was president of the WASP (Women Airforce Service Pilots of WWII). Under the guidance of Retired Col. Bruce Arnold, son of WWII General "Hap" Arnold, we lobbied Congress to provide the militarization denied us in 1944. This would grant us status as Veterans of WWII. Although we were successful, no formal acknowledgement was ever given.

Nancy Parrish, daughter of WASP Deanie Parrish and founder of Wings Across America (wingsacrossamerica.us) felt it was appropriate that Congress honor the accomplishments of the WASP. The Parrish's diligently sought congressional recognition since 2007. They contacted Air Force Major Nicole Malachowski, the first female Thunderbird pilot, for help and she took the lead. In January of 2009 she drafted a bill to award the Congressional Gold Medal to the WASP -- the highest honor awarded to a civilian by the United States Congress.

Senators Kay Bailey Hutchison (R-TX) and Barbara Mikulski (D-MD) introduced Senate Bill S614 in March 2009. The bill passed unanimously in May 2009.

House Representatives Ileana Ros-Lehtinen (R-FL) and Susan Davis (D-CA) introduced HR 2014 in April 2009, which also passed unanimously in June 2009.

Our heartfelt thanks to ALL Congress Members for rectifying the wrong that had been done in 1944 at which time the WASP had been denied militarization. We appreciate the recognition of our service to our country although of the original 1102 fewer than 300 remain.

## THE ALL WOMEN'S CLASSIC AIR RACE

Susan King, Co-founder and Managing Director of Wings of Dreams Museum, (wingsofdreams.org) Keystone Heights Airport, Keystone, Florida invited me to be part of a team entering the All Women's Classic Race.

Christy Smith of Jacksonville, Florida piloted the Diamond Star DA40XL aircraft; Susan was co-pilot, and 88 year old Bee Haydu was the backseat pilot. The race started June 23, 2009 in Denver, CO and after nine stops, 2700+ miles, ended in Atlantic, Iowa. Coincidentally, the second stop was Avenger Field in Sweetwater, Texas where the WASP had trained. It was 110 degrees. We had four days to finish. However we completed the race in 2 days. Although we were the first to land, we did not win. Being the first means nothing in this type of race as scoring is based on the handicap of each plane and pilots choice as to when to fly.

After the race, we departed from Atlantic, Iowa on June 29 to return the plane to Keystone Heights Airport, Florida. En route, we were fueling in Macon, GA when Nancy Parrish called my cell phone asking if I could be in the Oval Office of the White House by 4 pm the next day, to witness the President sign a bill awarding WASP The Congressional Gold Medal. GULP!!!

We returned our race plane to Keystone Heights, FL where, fortunately, Christy Smith had left her plane. We then flew to her home in Jacksonville, Florida. I purchased a commercial airline ticket for DC for the next morning. I MADE IT!

## THE OVAL OFFICE

All of us attending the Oval Office signing met outside the White House. We passed two security points where our credentials were carefully checked. We entered the White House by a western entrance and were escorted to the Roosevelt Room, adjacent to the Oval Office. When our turn, the door opened and much to my surprise we were greeted by President Obama who had something complimentary to say to each of us. We stood behind his desk and chair to witness the signing. The desk is the same one that had been used by President Kennedy. As President Obama approached, I had the pleasure of pulling out his chair for him. He appreciated that so I pulled it out again after he signed the bill. He used 4 pens to sign and gave each of the 3 WASP one. The other he gave to Rep. Ileana Ros-Lehtinen.

President Obama said, "Every American should be grateful for their service, and I am honored to sign this bill to finally give them some of the hard-earned recognition they deserve." We visited for about 10 minutes when he had to leave. He is a very gracious gentleman.

**This "Once In A Lifetime" experience will keep me on
Cloud Nine for the rest of my life.**

*President Barack Obama signs S.614, a bill to award a Congressional Gold Medal to the Women Airforce Service Pilots, in the Oval Office Wednesday, July 1, 2009. Flanking the President are Bernice Falk Haydu, far left, Elaine Danforth Harmon, and Lorraine H. Rodgers, right, Rep. Ileana Ros-Lehtinen (R-Fla.). Behind the President are active duty US Air Force pilots. Far right is Nicole Malachowski, the first woman to fly with the Air Force Air Demonstration Squadron, the Thunderbirds.*

*June 25, 2009 Atlantic, Iowa, Terminus of Air Classic Race. Christy Smith, pilot; Bee Haydu, back seat pilot; Susan King, co-pilot celebrate in front of their Diamond Star DA40XL – the first to land.*

RECEIVING MY MEDAL

*March 10, 2010 Tsgt. Susan Mayer, my escort, presented me with the medal. Looking on, my daughter Diana Potter and her husband Jeffrey, his brother Fred and my son Joseph. Other than receiving my WASP wings Sept. 8, 1944, some 65 years ago, this was one of the most rewarding events of my life.*

THE CONGRESSIONAL GOLD MEDAL

*Look closely at the side of the medal that has WASP figures. Note the female figures crossing the line. That is symbolic of what the WASP accomplished. They crossed the line that had been set up in an attempt to deny women the opportunity to fly military aircraft.*
*\*This is the highest honor given by the Congress*

# Letters Home
# 1944-1945

**A Must Book for Aviation History Buffs**

**AND**

**A Great Gift for Children and Grandchildren**

Individual or quantity pricing available.

**For information: beehaydu@beehaydu.com**

**Website: www.wasplettershome.com**